GOD AMONG US

The Rational Case for The Incarnation

SAMEH SAIED

LOGOS ECHOES

CONTENTS

Preface
Introduction

Part One
Divine Encounter :
The Role of Incarnation in Understanding God and Humanity

Part Two
The Incarnation:
Understanding Divine Union, Son-ship, And the Church

Part Three
Understanding the Christian Doctrine of Incarnation: Distinctions, Development, and Context

Epilogue

Navigating Faith and Community:
Principles for a Transformative Christian Journey

About LOGOS ECHOES Publications
About the Author

THE WORD BECAME FLESH
AND MADE HIS DWELLING AMONG US.
WE HAVE SEEN HIS GLORY,
THE GLORY OF THE ONE AND ONLY SON,
WHO CAME FROM THE FATHER, FULL OF
GRACE AND TRUTH.

JOHN 1:14

The Incarnation:
The Living Logos Beyond Written Texts

The Incarnation is central to Christianity. Since God revealed Himself through human nature, it was necessary for the four Gospels to offer different perspectives on Christ. The Gospels reflect the experiences of those who lived with Christ, and thus each Gospel writer presents a unique view of His life.

If God had revealed Himself solely through a written text, such a revelation would be limited to the written word. Words, no matter how profound, have inherent limitations and often require interpretation, and sometimes even further interpretation. There is a significant difference between the written word and a person. If words were clearer than a person, they would become the law and the guiding principle for humanity. If the law were clearer than a person, it would ultimately mean that humanity could not understand the law.

St. Clement of Alexandria remarked, "*The Jews take pride in the prophets, the Greeks in philosophy. The former take pride in the law, the latter in knowledge. But we, if we wish to boast, should boast in life.*" (*Stromata*, 1, 1). This life produces true knowledge. Written words can change or become obsolete; if they do not change, they become stagnant. Life, however, grows and evolves naturally into something better. Thus, Christian doctrine gains new dimensions over time because it is rooted in the life of Christ.

This is what St. Paul meant when he said that the letter is old, but the spirit is new, and thus we worship God not with the old letter but with the new spirit (2 Cor. 3:6). Christianity did not introduce an earthly law. The Incarnation is a significant call to return spirituality (the relationship with God) to human nature.

In other words, if we seek God, we should not look for Him in the cosmos, which only reveals God's power. Similarly, we should not search for Him outside humanity, as God outside humanity reveals His wisdom. Instead, we should seek God within humanity. Searching for God outside humanity reflects the remnants of human fallenness, as humanity, after the fall, searched for God outside itself because its life had dried up and God no longer shone within it as clearly as before the fall. A person searching for God outside their own life will not find God; they may find His power or wisdom, but not God as a person who interacts with humanity on a personal level. Therefore, we do not find God in the cosmos but in Jesus Christ.

As Christians, we believe in the new life that Christ brought. This new life cannot be conveyed through written words. This is what St. Paul addressed regarding the law; the law is good and holy, and the commandment is righteous, but it cannot bring the dead to life (Rom. 7:12). The distinction between the Old and New Testaments is that in the Old Testament, the law served as the mediator between God and humanity, while in the New Testament, Christ is the mediator (Heb.8:6). In the New Testament, Christ has replaced the Torah and the law. Hence, we can discuss the resurrection of the dead, the restoration of sight to the blind, and the release of the captives from the bondage of sin (Luke. 4:18; John. 11:43-44)

The law imposed the penalty of death on humanity, but the essence of Christianity is that God restores life to humanity. Thus, the dead person who receives life from God can live at a much higher level than what the law and the Old Testament commandments offer. Consequently, the profound doctrinal principles stated on the mountain can only be understood through the fact that Christ is the mediator of the New Covenant who brings new life (Matt. 5-7).

Anyone who receives this new life will experience peace, purity of heart, humility, and love for others. The commandments such as "*If anyone compels you to go one mile, go with him two*" (Matt. 5:41), "*If anyone wants to take your tunic, let him have your cloak also*" (Matt. 5:40), "*If anyone strikes you on the right cheek*" (Matt .5:39), etc., are not directives given to humans imprisoned by death who have decayed human lives but to those with a renewed human life.

Therefore, it is essential when reading the Gospel to understand that it is not merely written words; "*The words I speak to you are spirit and life*" (John.6:63). The spirit and life are testified by the Gospel. The Incarnation is the union of divinity with humanity; it encompasses the cross, the resurrection, the ascension, and sitting at the right hand of the Father. The incarnate God, who united with human nature, significantly transformed that nature. The Feast of the Epiphany, or the Feast of the Baptism of Christ, represents the beginning of Christ's revelation as the Son of God, and on this feast, we received our name as Christians because Christ was anointed with the Holy Spirit, and we share in that anointing (Luke.3:21-22). Everything that happens to Christ happens to us; nothing in our spiritual life can originate from ourselves but begins in Christ, who is the firstborn among many brothers (Rom.8:29). If we possess abilities not found in Christ, they will not endure and will lack life-giving power. If there are abilities present in Christ but not in us, it indicates a flaw, either in our teaching or spiritual life. Christ accepted the Holy Spirit on behalf of humanity. The eternal Son, who is eternally one with the Father and the Holy Spirit, does not need the Holy Spirit and cannot be anointed with it, but when He became incarnate and human like us, He was anointed with the Holy Spirit for our sake.

The forgiveness we received through Christ's baptism in the Jordan, as explained by the Church Fathers, is the restoration of the Holy Spirit to human nature. Christian teaching on forgiveness involves not only lifting the penalty of death but also renewing human nature, healing the soul and body, and restoring humanity to the fellowship of the Church (Acts. 3:19). Therefore, it is crucial not to think that a person who sins after baptism is like Adam after the fall.

The Lord Jesus Christ removed the penalty of death forever through His death (Heb. 9:26). Thus, we who have been baptized and accepted the faith do not stand before the Father as those punished with the penalty of death but as sick needing healing. Hence, St. James the Apostle says, "*If anyone has committed sin... the prayer of faith will heal the sick*" (Jas.5:15). Sin here might represent a disease needing healing, ignorance needing teaching, or corruption needing renewal through the Eucharist and repentance.

We do not return to being like Adam after the fall because Christ condemned sin in the flesh and defeated death through His death. This is the profound change brought by the Incarnation. The mediator is now alive forever, possessing an indestructible power of life: "*Now may the God of peace who brought up our Lord Jesus from the dead, that great Shepherd of the sheep, through the blood of the everlasting covenant*" (Heb.13:20). Therefore, the power and gifts of the cross reach us through the resurrection. The high priest who offered this sacrifice once for all did not die like the high priests of the Old Testament but lives forever and appears before the Father's face for us (Heb.7:24-25). By His Incarnation, Christ transferred human nature to a state of incorruption, uniting with all aspects of human nature, namely the soul and body. Thus, we must understand that everything that comes to humanity in the new life is through the Incarnation. Outside the Incarnation, there is nothing we can request from the Father. Everything we ask for, we ask in the new head of humanity, the second Adam, the Lord from heaven (1 Cor. 15:45).

<u>Note:</u> Throughout this book, you may notice a few recurring references to biblical passages and the writings of Church Fathers. These repetitions are intentional and designed to deepen your understanding of the subject matter. Each recurrence offers fresh insights, revealing new connections and applications within the broader context of the text.

Introduction

God Among Us: The Rational Case for the Incarnation embarks on a profound and exhaustive exploration of one of Christianity's most central and distinctive doctrines: the Incarnation. This doctrine, which posits that God became human through the person of Jesus Christ, occupies a pivotal place at the heart of Christian faith. It offers a unique and compelling perspective on the relationship between the divine and humanity, revealing how the infinite and the finite intersect in the most remarkable and transformative manner. This book is dedicated to unravelling and rationalizing this profound belief, providing a comprehensive understanding of how the divine can assume human form and what this revelation signifies for our grasp of both divinity and human nature.

The Incarnation asserts that Jesus Christ embodies both divine and human natures in perfect unity. This assertion is not merely a theological tenet but a profound declaration about the nature of God and His interaction with creation. It challenges the traditional notions of God as a distant, abstract force and instead presents a vision of a God who is intimately involved in the human experience. Through the Incarnation, God demonstrates that divine love and commitment are not abstract ideals but tangible realities that are lived out in the everyday experiences of human life. This act of divine involvement and engagement underscores a profound relational dynamic that redefines how we understand and experience the divine presence in our world.

The implications of the Incarnation extend well beyond its theological foundations. It introduces deep philosophical questions that challenge conventional views of divinity and human existence.

By embodying divine attributes within a finite human form, the Incarnation confronts us with a paradox that stretches the limits of human understanding.

How can the infinite nature of God coexist with the finite constraints of human existence? This paradox invites a re-evaluation of our concepts of greatness, power, and the essence of reality. It stimulates a profound reflection on how the divine can interact with and be present within the limitations of the created world, pushing the boundaries of human intellectual and spiritual exploration.

This book argues that the Incarnation is not simply a theological abstraction but a logical and coherent extension of divine love and wisdom. It explores how this doctrine harmonizes with fundamental Christian beliefs about creation, sin, and redemption, providing a narrative that integrates these core aspects of faith into a unified understanding of God's plan for humanity. The historical development of the doctrine—shaped by the insights of early Church Fathers, the deliberations of pivotal councils, and the theological debates that have evolved over centuries—demonstrates the complexity and depth of this belief. The Incarnation has been continually defended and refined throughout Christian history, reflecting its enduring significance and its pivotal role within the broader framework of Christian theology.

The implications of the Incarnation are vast and far-reaching. It offers a solid foundation for understanding God's active role in human life and provides a model of empathy and relational engagement that is central to the Christian experience. The belief that God has lived and suffered as a human being provides believers with a profound sense of connection and assurance of God's personal and intimate relationship with them. This belief influences not only how believers understand and practice worship but also shapes their ethical perspectives and daily lives. It affirms the inherent value and dignity of human existence, encouraging a worldview that is both meaningful and filled with hope.

By delving into these various dimensions, *God Among Us: The Rational Case for the Incarnation* aims to present a thorough and reasoned exploration of why the Incarnation is a rational and coherent element of Christian belief.

Through a detailed examination of theological, historical, and philosophical perspectives, this book seeks to provide a rich and nuanced understanding of the Incarnation and its profound implications for both faith and reason. It invites readers to engage with the doctrine in a way that deepens their appreciation of its significance and its impact on their spiritual and intellectual lives.

The first part , *"Divine Encounter: The Role of Incarnation in Understanding God and Humanity,"* initiates our journey by addressing the Incarnation as a pivotal divine revelation through human nature. This part probes the essence of how God's unity intersects with human limitations, presenting the Incarnation not merely as a theological concept but as a profound act of divine communication. It examines how the Incarnation serves as a bridge between the infinite truths of the divine and the finite expressions of human language, thereby providing a new lens through which we can view divine love and the divine image. This section also explores how the Incarnation reshapes our relationship with God, offering insights into how humanity itself becomes a reflection of a divine project through this sacred union.

In the second part, *"The Incarnation: Understanding Divine Union, Sonship, and the Church,"* the focus shifts to the multifaceted implications of the Incarnation for the nature of divine relationship and its impact on the Christian Church. This part delves into the reasons behind the necessity of the Incarnation, highlighting the transformative gift of son-ship and its implications for how we approach and relate to the incarnate God. It explores the complexities of divine relationship and prayer, emphasizing how the Incarnation redefines our spiritual interactions and the transformation of humanity's relationship with God. Additionally, this part reflects on the eternal nature of the Incarnation, examining its role in the formation and understanding of the Church as the body of Christ, including the sacramental significance of the Eucharist.

The third part , *"Understanding the Christian Doctrine of Incarnation: Distinctions, Development, and Context,"* provides a comprehensive analysis of the Christian doctrine of the Incarnation within its broader historical and theological context.

This part critiques the limitations of linguistic and conceptual similarities in understanding the Incarnation, exploring the theological distinctions that set the Christian perspective apart from other religious and philosophical traditions. It traces the development of the doctrine through historical and philosophical lenses, examining its continuity and divergence from Jewish and pagan thought. By addressing the interplay between rationality, faith, and prayer, this part aims to clarify how the doctrine of the Incarnation integrates into the broader tapestry of Christian belief.

Through this thorough examination, *God Among Us* seeks to offer readers a rational and profound understanding of the Incarnation, presenting it as a vital element of Christian theology that bridges the gap between the divine and the human. By engaging with the complexities of this doctrine, the book aims to enhance our comprehension of its implications for Christian faith and practice, and to provide a richer appreciation of its role in shaping our understanding of both God and humanity.

PART ONE
DIVINE ENCOUNTER :
THE ROLE OF INCARNATION IN UNDERSTANDING GOD AND HUMANITY

This part , titled *"Divine Encounter: The Role of Incarnation in Understanding God and Humanity,"* delves deeply into how the Incarnation reveals and shapes our understanding of both God and humanity.

We commence with *"The Doctrine of Incarnation: Divine Revelation Through Human Nature,"* setting the groundwork for our exploration by highlighting how the Incarnation serves as a direct and transformative revelation of the divine through the medium of human nature. This doctrine encapsulates how God, in His infinite transcendence, chose to reveal Himself within the confines of human experience, thereby making the divine accessible and tangible.

Following this, *"Understanding the Incarnation: Divine Unity and Human Limitations"* provides insight into the intricate relationship between the infinite unity of the divine and the finite limitations of human nature. This discussion illuminates the remarkable synthesis of these dimensions within the Incarnation, illustrating how divine unity and human frailty coexist in this profound mystery.

In *"The Nature of Divine Revelation: Bridging Human Language and Eternal Truths,"* we examine how the Incarnation acts as a bridge between the limitations of human language and the boundless truths of the divine. This section reveals how the Incarnation translates eternal divine realities into a form that can be comprehended and engaged with by human beings.

The section then turns to *"The Incarnation and the Role of the Bible,"* exploring how scriptural accounts of the Incarnation provide a foundational narrative that shapes our theological understanding and spiritual reflections. We assess the Bible's role in framing the Incarnation and its implications for Christian faith.

"The Incarnation and Divine Love" delves into how the Incarnation epitomizes and expresses the depth of divine love. This segment reflects on how the act of God becoming human is an ultimate demonstration of His love for humanity, offering a tangible expression of His commitment and compassion.

In *"The Incarnation and the Divine Image,"* we consider how the Incarnation reaffirms the concept of humanity being created in the image of God. This discussion highlights how the divine nature is mirrored in human form and what this means for our identity and purpose.

"Humanity as a Divine Project" examines the idea that humanity is integral to God's divine plan, with the Incarnation being a central element in this redemptive project. This section underscores the significance of the Incarnation in the context of God's overarching design for humanity.

We then explore *"The Incarnation and Our Relationship with God,"* focusing on how the Incarnation transforms and enriches our relationship with the divine. This exploration provides insights into how the Incarnation reshapes our engagement with God on both personal and communal levels.

"Divine Love and the Majesty of God" offers a reflection on how the Incarnation reveals the balance between divine love and majesty. This section seeks to deepen our appreciation of the divine attributes as

they are expressed through the life and mission of Christ.

Finally, *"The Nature of the Divine-Human Relationship: Contrasts and Similarities"* investigates the dynamic interplay between the divine and human aspects of the Incarnation. This analysis aims to provide a nuanced understanding of how these two dimensions interact, highlighting both their contrasts and their profound connections.

Through this part, we aim to uncover the rich theological and existential implications of the Incarnation, providing a comprehensive understanding of its role in bridging the divine and human, and its impact on our perceptions of God and our own humanity.

The Doctrine of Incarnation: Divine Revelation Through Human Nature

In Christianity, the doctrine of incarnation is a distinguishing feature of faith in God. While various religions discuss God in one way or another, Christianity uniquely emphasizes God's profound and unparalleled love for humanity. This love led God to reveal Himself by assuming human nature, encompassing both spirit and body, thus manifesting Himself through a fully human life embodied in the person of Jesus Christ. This truth is underscored in the Gospel of Matthew, where it is written, *"Behold, the virgin shall conceive and bear a son, and they shall call his name Immanuel,"* which translates to *"God with us"* (Matt.1:23). This passage not only highlights the miraculous nature of Jesus's birth but also affirms the divine presence in human form. Similarly, the Gospel of John emphasizes the significance of this incarnation, stating, *"And the Word became flesh and dwelt among us"* (John. 1:14). This verse encapsulates the core of Christian belief in the embodiment of the divine Word in human flesh.

The concept of God's revelation in Christianity extends beyond the mere disclosure of attributes; it involves revealing His very essence. The doctrine of incarnation is central to this revelation. The question arises: why did God choose the incarnation as the means to fully reveal Himself, rather than merely communicating through words alone? Christianity acknowledges that God has communicated through prophets, as illustrated in the Epistle to the Hebrews: *"Long ago, at many times and in many ways, God spoke to our fathers by the prophets, but in these last days he has spoken to us by his Son"* (Heb.1:1-2). This passage indicates that revelation is more than divine communication; it is an active and intimate disclosure of God's nature.

Early Church Fathers provided profound insights into this doctrine. St. Clement of Alexandria, in his *Stromata* 1.7, compared *"revelation"* to *"betrothal"* and *"incarnation"* to *"marriage,"* suggesting that while betrothal signifies an initial connection, it is through marriage that a more profound union is realized.

He wrote, *"For revelation is not a mere promise, but an earnest of the marriage of the soul to the Divine"*. This metaphor illustrates that God's final revelation and full union with humanity are completed through the incarnation.

St. Irenaeus of Lyons, in *Against Heresies* 3. 18, emphasizes the necessity of the incarnation for restoring humanity. He states, *"Our Lord Jesus Christ, in order to restore that which was lost, did not disdain to come down to our low estate, and to share in our suffering"*. This highlights the incarnation's role in restoring and transforming humanity.

St. Athanasius of Alexandria provides a powerful explanation of the incarnation's necessity in *On the*

Incarnation 54. He argues, *"He became what we are that He might make us what He is"*. This statement underscores the transformative nature of the incarnation, emphasizing that Christ assumed human nature to elevate it to divine status.

In *Great Catechism* 15, St. Gregory of Nyssa reflects on the mystery of the incarnation, writing, *"The divine has become human not by leaving behind its own nature but by taking on the nature of humanity"*. This perspective emphasizes the coexistence of divine and human natures without mixing or altering each other.

Critics sometimes question whether the concept of God's interest in humanity is exaggerated. Exaggeration implies adding imaginative elements to enhance significance. However, it can be argued that nothing fanciful has been added to the actual reality of creation. Observing the natural world reveals that humanity appears to be the pinnacle of God's creation. This view is reflected in the Psalmist's wonder: *"What is man that you are mindful of him, and the son of man that you care for him? Yet you have made him a little lower than the heavenly beings and crowned him with glory and honour"* (Ps. 8:4-6). This passage underscores the special status of humanity within creation. From the majestic sun to the tiniest bacteria, everything seems designed to serve humanity, affirming that humans hold a central place in the created order.

Thus, recognizing the greatness of humanity and the significance of God's choice to unite with human nature is not an exaggeration but a reflection of divine purpose.

The critique that incarnation represents divine condescension and undermines God's majesty often stems from subjective perspectives. Religious thought is sometimes influenced by personal viewpoints rather than objective standards. As the

Apostle Paul remarks in 1 Corinthians, *"For the word of the cross is folly to those who are perishing, but to us who are being saved it is the power of God... For the foolishness of God is wiser than men, and the weakness of God is stronger than men"*(1 Cor. 1:18-25). This passage suggests that rejecting the incarnation due to perceived unworthiness reflects a subjective view rather than an objective truth. St. Augustine of Hippo also addresses this in his *City of God* 22.29, where he reflects on the paradox of divine humility and majesty: *"The Lord of heaven and earth, becoming man, chose to be humble in His love, showing that even in His humility He is all-powerful"*

The common objection that God's greatness would preclude Him from becoming incarnate can be reconsidered. God's greatness might instead be expressed as a profound manifestation of love rather than aloofness. The Apostle Paul elaborates on this perspective in Philippians: *"But made himself nothing, taking the form of a servant, being born in the likeness of men. And being found in human form, he humbled himself by becoming obedient to the point of death, even death on a cross"* (Phil.2:7-8). This passage highlights the humility and depth of God's love demonstrated through the incarnation. St. Athanasius echoes this sentiment in *On the Incarnation 54*, emphasizing that the incarnation was an act of profound love and humility

Furthermore, the prophet Isaiah provides a perspective on God's ways and thoughts being higher than human understanding: *"For my thoughts are not your thoughts, neither are your ways my ways, declares the Lord. For as the heavens are higher than the earth, so are my ways higher than your ways and my thoughts than your thoughts"* (Isa. 55:8-9). This view challenges the notion that divine greatness would necessarily exclude the possibility of incarnation.

It suggests that God's ways transcend human limitations, and His actions, including the incarnation, reflect a higher, more profound understanding of love and engagement with creation.

In exploring the implications of the incarnation, it is also important to consider its impact on Christian theology and human experience. The doctrine of incarnation asserts that God has entered into the human condition in its entirety, not only to reveal divine nature but to transform and redeem it. This transformative aspect is reflected in the New Testament, where the Apostle John writes, *"But to all who did receive him, who believed in his name, he gave the right to become children of God"* (John.1:12). This indicates that through the incarnation, believers are invited into a new relationship with God, characterized by divine son-ship and participation in the divine nature. St. Irenaeus, in *Against Heresies* 5.1, elaborates on this, stating, *"Through the incarnation, we are not only saved from our sins but are made partakers of the divine nature"*

The incarnation also invites believers to understand God's engagement with humanity in terms of empathy and solidarity. Jesus, as described in Hebrews 4:15, *"For we do not have a high priest who is unable to sympathize with our weaknesses, but one who in every respect has been tempted as we are, yet without sin."* This passage emphasizes that Jesus' humanity allows Him to fully understand and empathize with human experiences and struggles, bridging the gap between the divine and the human. St. Gregory of Nazianzus, in *Oration* 30. 5 addresses this aspect: *"In His human nature, Christ experienced all that we endure, not merely to observe, but to genuinely sympathize and transform our suffering"*

In summary, the doctrine of incarnation in Christianity is not merely a theological concept but a profound expression of divine love and engagement with humanity. It reveals God's willingness to enter into human experience fully, while remaining divine, to bring about a deeper understanding of His nature and to transform human existence.

Understanding the Incarnation: Divine Unity and Human Limitations

In exploring the doctrine of incarnation in Christianity, it is crucial to understand that this doctrine does not imply a transformation of God into a human. Christian teaching asserts that God's essence remains unaltered even as He assumes human nature. This profound union of divine and human natures is central to Christian faith and is supported by numerous scriptural passages and theological interpretations from the Early Church Fathers.

The Gospel of Matthew underscores the significance of the incarnation with the prophecy in Matthew 1:23: *"Behold, the virgin shall conceive and bear a son, and they shall call his name Immanuel,"* which translates to *"God with us."* This prophecy is not merely a prediction but a profound statement of God's intention to enter into human history and experience in a tangible way. The name *"Immanuel"* signifies God's presence within the human realm, highlighting the deep connection between the divine and human.

Similarly, the Gospel of John articulates the incarnation by stating, *"And the Word became flesh and dwelt among us"* (John 1:14). This verse is central to Christian understanding of the incarnation, emphasizing that Jesus is the divine Word made manifest in human form. The term *"Word"* (Logos) represents the pre-existent divine reason or creative order, which took on human nature to bridge the gap between the infinite God and finite humanity. This encapsulates the transformative impact of the incarnation, suggesting that through Christ's humanity, humanity itself is elevated.

Addressing objections to the incarnation involves considering several critical issues. One major objection is that God's nature is fundamentally different from human nature, implying an insurmountable barrier to their union. However, Christian theology holds that despite the fundamental differences between God and humans, God's omnipotence enables Him to transcend these differences without compromising His divine essence.

Another objection concerns the limitations of humanity. Critics argue that if God were to become human, He would be subject to human frailties and constraints. This objection is countered by the belief that divine essence is not confined by human limitations. The creation of the universe serves as evidence of God's ability to be present both within and beyond creation. Just as God created and upholds the cosmos while remaining transcendent, He can unite with human nature without being confined by it. As St. Gregory of Nyssa writes in *Great Catechism* 15: *"The Word of God, by becoming flesh, united Himself to us, so that the division between humanity and divinity might be healed."* This perspective emphasizes that the incarnation serves to heal the rift between humanity and divinity, rather than confining God's essence.

The third objection involves the perceived lowliness of human actions such as eating, drinking, and excretion. Critics argue that such bodily functions are unworthy of the Creator. This view overlooks the intricate design and purpose of creation. St. Gregory of Nyssa, in *On the Making of Man* 10, reflects on the significance of human creation: *"The body is not an instrument of degradation but a divine creation with a purpose and honour."* This understanding shows that human experiences and functions are part of a divine plan that reflects God's creativity and glory.

The critique that incarnation is unworthy of God can be challenged by recognizing that divine nature is not constrained by human psychological limitations. Misconceptions or biases might create a disconnect between divine and human understanding.

In discussing the creation of humanity, the biblical account affirms that God created humans from clay and endowed them with an eternal soul. Genesis 2:7 states, *"Then the Lord God formed the man of dust from the ground and breathed into his nostrils the breath of life, and the man became a living creature."* This narrative underscores humanity's unique role and honour in creation, distinguishing humans from angels and emphasizing their favoured status. St. Irenaeus of Lyons, in *Against Heresies* 5.16, states: *"For this is the reason why the Word of God became man, to restore man to the glory that was lost through sin."* This perspective reinforces the idea that the incarnation is central to restoring and elevating humanity's original dignity.

The conversation on incarnation concludes with an examination of God's expression of love. Love, as a divine attribute, can be expressed in various ways, including through revelation. St. Cyril of Alexandria, in *Third Letter to Nestorius.* 8, further supports this view: *"Our Lord Jesus Christ is one, not in the sense of a divided nature but in the union of the divine and human natures in one person."* This understanding emphasizes that revelation through the incarnation is profound expression of divine love and commitment to humanity, embodying the ultimate bridge between God and human beings.

The doctrine of incarnation in Christianity thus emerges not merely as a theological concept but as a profound manifestation of divine love and engagement with humanity. It reveals God's willingness to fully enter human experience while maintaining His divine nature, thereby deepening the understanding of His nature and transforming human existence. Through a detailed examination of scriptural references and theological perspectives from Early Church Fathers, the significance of the incarnation as a cornerstone of Christian faith becomes clear, illustrating its profound impact on understanding God's relationship with humanity.

The Nature of Divine Revelation: Bridging Human Language and Eternal Truths

The interpretation that divine revelation consists of human words might initially seem unconventional, but it underscores a profound understanding of the nature of revelation itself. In religious traditions, divine revelation is conveyed through human language to ensure it is intelligible and accessible to humanity. If divine revelation were expressed in a celestial language, beyond human comprehension, it would be inaccessible and create a significant barrier to understanding. Thus, the necessity of using human language for revelation is paramount to its effectiveness and relevance.

The notion that divine revelation is articulated through human language because it is intended for human understanding is well-supported by biblical texts. In the Apostle Paul's letters, we find a clear explanation of this concept. In 1 Corinthians 2:10-13, Paul writes, *"These things God has revealed to us through the Spirit. For the Spirit searches everything, even the depths of God. For who knows a person's thoughts except the spirit of that person, which is in him? So also no one comprehends the thoughts of God except the Spirit of God. Now we have received not the spirit of the world, but the Spirit who is from God, that we might understand the things freely given us by God. And we impart this in words not taught by human wisdom but taught by the Spirit, interpreting spiritual truths to those who are spiritual"* (1 Cor. 2:10-13). Paul emphasizes that the Spirit enables the comprehension of divine truths through human language, ensuring that these revelations are understandable and pertinent to human experience.

This view is echoed by the Early Church Fathers who consistently affirmed that divine revelation must be communicated in a way that human beings can grasp. St. Augustine of Hippo, in *On Christian Doctrine* 2. 1, elaborates on the necessity of human language for the understanding of divine truths. Augustine notes, *"We do not think that the things that are written are to be understood as if they had been said in some celestial tongue... but we acknowledge that they are meant to be understood by those who are in the church"*. This perspective highlights that divine messages are intentionally adapted to human language to facilitate comprehension within the cultural and linguistic context of its audience.

Furthermore, Origen of Alexandria, a significant early Christian theologian, discusses the communication of divine messages through human language in his *Commentary on the Gospel of John* 1.1. Origen asserts, *"The divine words are spoken in a way that is adapted to our capacity for understanding... they are communicated to us through our own language, which is the only means available to us"*. This acknowledgment of the use of human language reinforces the idea that divine messages are intended to be accessible to human beings within their own cultural and linguistic contexts.

The idea that revelation is the beginning of divine interaction with humanity, rather than its entirety, is an important aspect to consider. Revelation, as understood in Christian theology, serves as a foundational step in establishing a relationship between God and humans. This perspective is supported by biblical texts that suggest further divine communication beyond the initial revelation.

For example, in the Gospel of John, Jesus states, *"I still have many things to say to you, but you cannot bear them now"* (John. 16:12). This indicates that divine communication is an on-going process, with the possibility of additional revelation beyond what is initially conveyed.

The temporal limitations of revelation highlight the challenge of reconciling divine messages with the evolving nature of human language. As languages change, terms used in revelation can become outdated and lose their original meaning. For instance, political systems have evolved, rendering terms like "king" less relevant, while technological advancements have replaced terms like "sword" with "rifle" and "camel" with "car" or "airplane." These changes illustrate how human language, and by extension, revelation expressed through it, can become disconnected from contemporary realities. Tertullian, an early Church Father, addresses this temporal nature of language in his work *On the Flesh of Christ* 7 stating, *"The words of Scripture are bound by the limits of human language, which is subject to change over time... thus, the eternal truth is communicated through temporal means"*.

This issue of reconciling the eternal nature of divine messages with the temporal nature of human language is significant. Although revelation aims to convey eternal truths, the words used are subject to change and may eventually lose their relevance. Modern linguistic studies, including morphology, analyse the evolution of language and the context in which terms were used. This underscores the importance of understanding the historical and cultural backdrop of the language to accurately grasp its intended meanings.

The discussion on revelation extends to other religious texts as well. The Bible, divided into the Old Testament and the New Testament, reflects a transition from understanding God through the Law to experiencing God as a living, human presence. The Old Testament primarily consists of the writings of the prophets, while the New Testament includes the accounts of those who lived with Christ and documented His life. The difference between the two Testaments illustrates a shift in divine communication from legal and prophetic to personal and incarnate.

This shift is reflected in the New Testament's portrayal of Jesus as a direct revelation of God. St. Irenaeus of Lyons, in *Against Heresies* 3.11 notes, *"The New Testament provides a more direct and personal revelation of God, manifesting His presence in a way that is closer to human experience"*. This view underscores the significance of the incarnation as a means of making divine revelation more immediate and relevant to human beings.

In summary, the concept that divine revelation is conveyed through human language highlights the necessity for effective communication with humanity. Through various scriptural references and the writings of early Church Fathers, we see that while divine revelation aims to be eternal and universal, it is articulated through human means to ensure comprehension and relevance. The transition from Old to New Testament further emphasizes the evolution of divine communication, offering a fuller and more accessible understanding of God's engagement with humanity.

The Incarnation and the Role of the Bible

The question of whether the Bible's role ceases once a person comes to know Christ requires a nuanced understanding of the Bible's purpose and significance in the life of a Christian. The assertion that the Bible's role extends beyond mere acquaintance with Christ is supported by the belief that the Bible is a source of divine wisdom and guidance not only for the present life but also for preparing believers for the ultimate vision of God in the afterlife. The concept that the Bible's relevance does not end with knowledge of Christ, but rather continues as an essential guide, is reflected in various scriptural passages and the writings of the Early Church Fathers.

Christian doctrine affirms that humanity will indeed see God on the Day of Judgment. This belief is rooted in various scriptural passages, such as Matthew 5:8, which states, *"Blessed are the pure in heart, for they shall see God."* This vision of God is not merely a metaphorical or symbolic sight but a direct and personal encounter with the divine presence. The idea that the incarnation, or God's becoming human, is inherently paradoxical is often debated. Some argue that if humanity is destined to see God directly, the necessity of the incarnation might seem redundant. However, the incarnation is understood as an essential part of God's plan for salvation and revelation, facilitating a profound and personal relationship with humanity.

The value of seeing God goes beyond mere material fulfillment in the afterlife. Critics who argue that eternal life should be sufficient, irrespective of divine knowledge, overlook the essence of divine interaction. The ultimate goal of human existence is not merely to possess material blessings but to engage in a meaningful relationship with God. Psalm 73:25-26 reflects this sentiment, *"Whom have I in heaven but You? And there is nothing on earth that I desire besides You. My flesh and my heart may fail, but God is the strength of my heart and my portion forever."* This passage underscores that true fulfilment comes from knowing and being with God rather than from material possessions alone.

The idea that the incarnation might be impossible while believing in an afterlife reflects a paradox. The belief in an afterlife and the vision of God suggests that God's ultimate purpose for humanity includes direct communion with Him, making the incarnation a means to achieve this end rather than a contradiction of it.

St. Augustine, in his *City of God* 1.1 emphasizes that the ultimate goal of human existence is to know and be united with God. He writes, *"Our hearts are restless until they find their rest in You"*. This statement underscores that the ultimate fulfilment of human life is found in the knowledge and vision of God, rather than in material blessings or earthly gains. For Augustine, the purpose of human creation is intrinsically linked to the relationship with God, making the vision of God essential to human purpose.

Critics who argue that material blessings should suffice in heaven miss the essence of divine interaction, which transcends mere material fulfilment. St. Irenaeus articulates this perspective in *Against Heresies* 4.20 stating, *"The glory of God is a living man; and the life of man consists in beholding God"*. This quote highlights that true fulfilment and the ultimate purpose of human life lie in the direct knowledge of God, rather than in the accumulation of material possessions. The idea that material abundance alone could satisfy human existence overlooks the deeper purpose of divine communion.

The ultimate disaster of an eternal state devoid of divine knowledge, even if surrounded by material blessings, would be a state of perpetual frustration and emptiness, as the true fulfilment of existence is found in the relationship with God.

The belief that God would create humanity only to withhold knowledge of Himself contradicts the nature of a benevolent Creator. St. Gregory of Nyssa, in his *Great Catechism* 3 asserts, *"The purpose of our creation is to be in communion with the divine nature"*. This assertion reinforces the idea that God's act of creation includes the desire for humanity to know and commune with Him. Denying this knowledge would be inconsistent with the notion of a just and benevolent Creator.

The concept of worshiping God is often misunderstood as a mere act of servitude. However, St. John Chrysostom, in his homilies, argues that true worship is not about outward acts but about the inward affections of the heart. He states, *"True worship is not in prostrations and outward acts, but in the inward affections of the heart"* (*Homilies on the Gospel of Matthew* 2). This emphasizes that worshiping God is about engaging in a meaningful relationship characterized by love rather than merely performing rituals. True love, which reflects divine nature, transcends servitude and embodies the unconditional and unwavering aspects of divine love.

St. Basil the Great echoes this sentiment in his Homilies, saying, *"Our love for God is a response to His love for us, and it is through this love that we come to know Him"* (*Homilies* 1). This perspective highlights that divine love is the ultimate expression of God's nature and is reflected in human relationships, such as those between family members and friends. The presence of love in human life mirrors the divine love and emphasizes the importance of knowing and relating to God.

In conclusion, the Bible's role extends beyond the initial acquaintance with Christ and continues as a vital source of guidance and preparation for the ultimate vision of God. The promise of seeing God, as affirmed in scripture and Early Church writings, underscores that the ultimate purpose of human existence is to know and be in relationship with the Creator. This relationship, characterized by love and fulfilment, highlights the on-going relevance of the Bible and the eternal significance of divine knowledge.

The insights from scriptural passages and Early Church Fathers provide a comprehensive understanding of the Bible's role in the believer's journey toward eternal communion with God.

The Incarnation and Divine Love

The nature of divine love as portrayed in Christian theology transcends ordinary human emotions. For example, in John 15:13, Jesus states, *"Greater love has no one than this: to lay down one's life for one's friends."* This sacrificial love is the epitome of divine love, characterized by selflessness and a willingness to endure suffering for the sake of others. This type of love is not merely an emotion but an active and purposeful commitment to the well-being of others. The Apostle Paul, in 1 Corinthians 13:4-7, further describes love as patient, kind, and not envious or boastful. These descriptions emphasize that love involves a deep, enduring commitment rather than transient emotions.

The incarnation illustrates this divine love by showing how God, through Christ, fully engages with human nature while maintaining His divine essence. This union is not about God becoming human in the literal sense of adopting human emotions or limitations but about God entering human history in a way that reveals His nature and purpose for humanity. This profound union allows for a complete depiction of human experience and emotion through the lens of divine love.

The understanding of love and incarnation often intersects with debates about divine and human greatness. If one acknowledges the greatness of God, it is essential to also recognize the significance of humanity within the divine plan. The relationship between divine greatness and human worth is integral to understanding both concepts fully. St. Irenaeus, in *Against Heresies* 3.20, writes, *"For this is the sum of the divine economy: the perfection of the invisible and the visible, the union of heaven and earth, and the gathering together of the children of God."* This reflection highlights that divine greatness is manifest in creation and human achievements.

Moreover, the denial of the incarnation can stem from a limited understanding of humanity's place in the divine order. St. Augustine of Hippo, in *Confessions* 7.10, emphasizes, *"You have made us for Yourself, and our hearts are restless until they rest in You."* This statement reflects the belief that humanity's ultimate purpose is to know and unite with God. To define God without acknowledging humanity's role in this divine scheme risks a diminished understanding of both.

In addressing the nature of divine love, it is essential to recognize that love is not merely an emotion but a profound expression of divine nature. The incarnation of Christ serves as a powerful example of this love, illustrating how God's interaction with humanity reflects His true nature. This understanding aligns with theological perspectives that emphasize the continuity between divine attributes and human experiences.

Thus, the exploration of love, incarnation, and the relationship between divine and human greatness requires a nuanced understanding of Christian theology. The Bible and early Church Fathers provide valuable insights into these concepts, affirming that divine love and the incarnation are integral to the Christian understanding of God's relationship with humanity. The teachings of the early Church Fathers, including St. Athanasius, St. Irenaeus, and St. Augustine, offer profound reflections on these themes, enriching our comprehension of divine love and the significance of the incarnation in Christian faith.

The Incarnation and the Divine Image

The concept of describing God in human terms often feels problematic, as it seems to limit the divine to human attributes. However, when discussing God, it is essential to use language that is comprehensible to human minds; otherwise, communication and even faith in God would become impossible. The suggestion that there is no difference between those who do not believe in God and those who refuse to describe Him highlights a critical issue: without a defined human nature, revelation would be inconceivable.

The very fact that revelation is possible implies a shared human experience that aligns with divine communication. In this context, the use of human language to describe divine attributes becomes a bridge between the finite human understanding and the infinite divine reality.

The incarnation fundamentally relies on the belief that the nature shared by all humans reflects the image of God. Although the term *"image of God"* might seem to diminish divine majesty, it actually underscores the grandeur of God. The concept of humanity reflecting the divine image signifies that human beings are a manifestation of God's glory and are considered God's representatives on Earth.

This notion finds its basis in scriptural texts and early Christian theological writings. In Genesis 1:26-27, we read: *"Then God said, 'Let us make man in our image, after our likeness.' So God created man in his own image, in the image of God he created him; male and female he created them."* This foundational passage asserts that humanity is created in the divine image, underscoring a profound connection between the Creator and the created.

The early Church Fathers echoed this understanding in their writings. St. Irenaeus of Lyons, in *Against Heresies*, 4.20 writes: *"For by the image of God I understand the perfect nature of man, through which the Creator has made him according to his own likeness"*. This reflects the view that the divine image in humanity signifies both the inherent dignity of human beings and their role as representatives of God on Earth.

While God is invisible, understanding God might be achieved through observing humanity. The *"image"* referred to here is not about physical resemblance but about qualities and capacities. Just as the universe reflects God's omnipotence, humanity reflects divine attributes in its nature and potential.

St. Gregory of Nyssa, in his *Great Catechism* 5 discusses how humanity's creation in God's image connects to divine intellect and purpose: *"Man, then, is said to be in the image of God, not in respect of his body, but in respect of the whole man's rational faculty"*. This view highlights that the divine image in humanity is about rationality, will, and moral potential rather than physical form.

The term *"image"* is significant for several reasons. First, it is based on divine revelation from

God Himself, as stated in Genesis. This term establishes a fundamental relationship between the visible and the invisible, connecting the material and spiritual realms. The essence of human existence and life is dependent on God, and discovering one's origin in God is crucial. In modern terms, humanity can be seen as the visible project that reveals the intellect of the divine Creator.

The value of this belief lies in the dynamic relationship between the image and its origin. Humanity, in striving to understand God, also discovers its own identity and future. Recognizing oneself in relation to God reveals a deeper understanding of one's nature and purpose. St. John Chrysostom, in his *Homilies on Matthew* 1 articulates this idea: *"The more you know about God, the more you know about yourself"*. This implies that understanding the divine image helps clarify human existence and destiny.

The discussion about the image of God does not imply that humans could become divine but rather emphasizes the distinction between creator and creation. The divine remains creator, and the created remains finite. The sensitivity to the term *"image"* might stem from a perception that it implies material or physical attributes, which are not applicable to God.

However, considering attributes like freedom, will, and intellect as elements of the divine image offers a more abstract but meaningful understanding. St. Cyril of Alexandria, in his *Commentary on John* 2 explains that while humanity reflects divine attributes, it remains distinct from divinity: *"He who sees Me sees the Father; He does not mean that the Father is identical with the Son but that the Son perfectly reveals the Father"*. This view highlights that the divine image in humanity reflects aspects of

God's nature without implying a physical or material equivalence.

The goal of human creation is growth and development, with the divine image serving as a model. The term "*image*" effectively captures the relationship between the material and spiritual worlds. Humanity is the link between these realms, embodying both material and spiritual elements. The resurrection of the body, regardless of its form, remains an integral aspect of human existence, affirming the connection between material and spiritual life. St. Gregory of Nazianzus, in his *Orations* 45 speaks of the resurrection as a fulfilment of the divine image: *"Christ has risen from the dead, and by rising has raised us up"*. This belief underscores that the material aspect of humanity is not separated from its spiritual dimension but is integral to its ultimate purpose.

Furthermore, the concept of the divine image explains the nature of prayer and worship. Humans are not praying to an unknown entity but seeking to reflect and emulate the divine origin that is evident in their own nature. It also clarifies the nature of good and evil, where failing to emulate God results in moral deviation, while true imitation leads to goodness. St. John Chrysostom, in *his Homilies on Matthew* 1 emphasizes that prayer and worship are acts of reflecting divine attributes: *"When you pray, you are approaching the divine nature itself, which is a reflection of divine goodness"*.

The belief in the divine image supports the equality of all humans in the eyes of God. Attacking any person is akin to assaulting the image of God, as indicated by scriptural teachings. This perspective elevates human dignity and underscores the moral gravity of disparaging others.

In his *Letter to Diognetus* 6 an early Christian apologist writes: *"The Christian has the same sort of relationship to the world as the soul has to the body"*, suggesting that all humans, as bearers of the divine image, are of inherent value and dignity.

Finally, the notion of the divine image illuminates the future relationship between God and humanity, explaining eternal life as an opportunity for the development of the divine image within humans. This belief deepens the communion between God and humanity, suggesting that eternal life is a recognition of the divine attributes imparted to humans. This perspective aligns with the notion that eternal life allows for the full realization of the divine image in humanity.

Thus, the concept of the divine image is central to Christianity. If any thinker were to dismantle this concept, it would not merely undermine Christianity but would fundamentally destroy the understanding of humanity itself.

Humanity as a Divine Project

Christianity presents a profound and expansive vision for humanity, asserting that God has endowed this project with every potential for success. This vision reflects a fundamental belief in the purpose and potential embedded within humanity, as illustrated by various biblical texts and early Christian writings. For instance, the creation of humanity in the divine image, as detailed in Genesis 1:26-27, affirms the intrinsic value and potential of human beings.

The passage states, *"Then God said, 'Let us make mankind in our image, in our likeness... So God created mankind in his own image, in the image of God he created them; male and female he created them."* This foundational scripture emphasizes that humanity reflects God's own image, suggesting a grand purpose and potential inherent in creation.

The idea that undermining this vision would imply either the existence of a superior alternative or an unconscious desire to dismantle humanity itself underscores the significance of thoroughly examining various religions to determine if there might be a more viable project than the one Christianity proposes. If an individual were to discover a more compelling alternative, they would be justified in reassessing their beliefs. The connection between the concept of humanity as the image of God and the doctrine of incarnation is significant. The incarnation, according to Christian belief, involves God taking on human form, signifying that the divine did not stray far from its essence but rather adopted a nature already aligned with His own. This belief is expressed in John 1:14, which states, *"The Word became flesh and made his dwelling among us."*

The notion of God's incarnation may seem challenging, especially if one perceives it as a deviation from the divine nature. However, Christian doctrine holds that this incarnation is not a denial of God's transcendence but an affirmation of His closeness to humanity. This understanding is supported by early Church Fathers such as St. Irenaeus, who argued in *Against Heresies* 3.16 that *"the Word of God, in His love for humanity, became what we are in order to make us what He is."*

This perspective emphasizes that the incarnation demonstrates God's intimate involvement with humanity rather than a departure from His divine nature.

God's sovereignty, as expressed through the incarnation, is not merely about power but about the transformative power of love. This assertion reflects the belief that the divine desire to overcome human sin is grounded in love rather than coercion. This form of sovereignty, characterized by love, contrasts with the tyrannical exercise of power. The concept of *"sovereignty of love"* challenges conventional associations of power with control and domination. True love, according to this perspective, is patient and persuasive rather than forceful.

This is exemplified by the story shared by St. John Chrysostom in his *Homilies on the Gospel of Matthew* 22, where he emphasized that *"The love of Christ is not coercive; it wins over the heart by its own virtue and sacrifice."*

In contrast, fear of punishment may influence behaviour but does not foster a genuine relationship with God. True relationship with the divine transcends mere fear and involves an understanding of God's nature and intentions. This is reflected in 1 John 4:18, which states, *"There is no fear in love. But perfect love drives out fear, because fear has to do with punishment. The one who fears is not made perfect in love."* The idea of God as a sovereign ruler and humanity as His subjects can take various forms, including manifestations of benevolence and compassion rather than mere dominance. In Christian theology, the relationship between God and humanity is one of mutual engagement rather than sheer control.

The incarnation reflects this understanding of divine sovereignty by demonstrating a willingness to engage with humanity in a transformative and loving manner. This engagement is not about exercising political power but about inviting humanity into a deeper relationship with the divine. The need for the incarnation is rooted in addressing human sinfulness and restoring the broken relationship between humanity and God. According to Christian doctrine, Adam's sin introduced death and corruption into the human experience, a condition inherited by subsequent generations. This concept is articulated in Romans 5:12, which states, *"Therefore, just as sin entered the world through one man, and death through sin, and in this way death came to all people, because all sinned."*

The concept of original sin does not imply that individuals inherit Adam's specific actions but rather the consequences of those actions. Just as a person's squandered wealth affects their descendants, Adam's sin resulted in a state of corruption and separation from God that affects all humanity. Humanity's quest for understanding its existence and identity reflects this condition. People are born with an inherent sense of separation from God, leading to existential questions about their purpose and existence.

This quest for meaning is described in Christian theology as *"the fall of Adam"* or *"the fall of humanity"*. The search for identity and purpose, even among the religious, illustrates the profound impact of this separation. It highlights the need for reconciliation with God as the source and reason for existence. In this view, humanity's existence is not self-sustained but is inherently connected to God. This perspective challenges the notion of complete individual autonomy, suggesting instead that every person is part of a larger, interconnected human experience. The interconnectedness of human existence means that individual actions and states of being have broader implications for others, reflecting a deeper unity within the human condition.

The idea that humans are not entirely independent but are dependent on God for their existence and purpose is central to Christian belief. This understanding underscores the importance of recognizing one's existence as rooted in the divine, providing a framework for understanding human purpose and the nature of the divine relationship. This acknowledgment of human dependence on God highlights the core of Christian existential understanding.

Thus, Christianity's expansive vision for humanity, encompassing the doctrine of incarnation and the concept of original sin, provides a framework for understanding human purpose and divine relationship. This vision asserts that God's project for humanity is not only viable but imbued with potential for success, challenging the notion of undermining this vision without considering the profound implications for both human existence and the divine plan.

The Incarnation and Our Relationship with God

Understanding God and the nature of divine-human relations reveals a deeply intricate and nuanced dynamic. It is possible for an individual to possess substantial knowledge about God without necessarily establishing a genuine, personal relationship with Him. This distinction is pivotal: having knowledge of God does not inherently guarantee the formation of a meaningful connection between the divine and humanity. True relationship goes beyond intellectual understanding and necessitates active engagement from both sides.

The relationship between God and humanity is fundamentally bilateral, meaning that it involves both parties actively participating in the connection. While human knowledge of God can provide valuable insights into His nature and attributes, it does not, on its own, ensure a deep, personal relationship. This relationship is not merely about intellectual comprehension; it is rooted in God's active involvement in fostering and nurturing the bond. Revelation plays a significant role in this context as it provides essential truths about God that guide human understanding. However, revelation alone does not, by itself, establish a profound and enduring relationship between humanity and God.

The distinction between *"knowledge"* and *"relationship"* is crucial here. Knowledge of God, while valuable, is not synonymous with a relationship. The essence of a genuine connection lies in the closeness and engagement of God with humanity. To illustrate this, consider the analogy of a great ruler who communicates through messages and directives but then retreats into silence. This analogy underscores how revelation, while informative, can fall short of establishing a direct and intimate connection. For instance, God's communication through the prophets in the Old Testament, such as Isaiah, who proclaimed, *"The Lord himself will give you a sign: The virgin will conceive and give birth to a son, and will call him Immanuel"* (Isa. 7:14, NIV), was significant but did not fully bridge the gap between humanity and the divine.

The repeated nature of these revelations indicates their limitations in fully connecting humanity with God. Thus, a more direct and intimate link between human life and divine life becomes essential. The inherent contrast between humanity and God is profound, yet there is also a relative similarity that makes revelation meaningful. If the contrast were absolute, the concept of revelation would seem futile. The divine concern for communicating with humanity, despite the differences, underscores the importance of establishing a relationship. This concern is reflected in John 3:16, which states, *"For God so loved the world that he gave his one and only Son, that whoever believes in him shall not perish but have eternal life."* This passage highlights God's motivation to reveal Himself for the purpose of relationship rather than mere information.

Just as a parent seeks to guide and correct their child out of love and responsibility, so too does God's revelation aim to bridge the gap between humanity and Himself, striving to build a meaningful relationship. This highlights the transformative nature of the divine-human relationship, aiming for more than mere knowledge.

This underscores the ultimate purpose of revelation and incarnation as fostering a relationship that allows humanity to share in the divine nature.

The concept of divine revelation as a means to establish and deepen a relationship is further exemplified in the New Testament. In the Gospels, Jesus often emphasized a personal relationship with God. For instance, in John 15:15, Jesus says, *"I no longer call you servants, because a servant does not know his master's business. Instead, I have called you friends, for everything that I learned from my Father I have made known to you."* This passage illustrates the transition from a mere servant relationship to one of intimacy and friendship, emphasizing the relational aspect of divine communication.

In summary, while knowledge of God through revelation is invaluable, it is the dynamic and relational engagement between humanity and God that forms the essence of a true and enduring connection.

The ultimate purpose of divine revelation is not solely to impart information but to build a transformative relationship that reflects God's deep concern and involvement in human life. This perspective is deeply embedded in the teachings of early Christian theologians and the New Testament, highlighting the importance of both knowledge and relationship in understanding the divine-human connection.

Divine Love and the Majesty of God

The topic of divine love often raises concerns about preserving the majesty of God. Some fear that emphasizing God's love might diminish His divine grandeur. However, such concerns overlook a crucial aspect: no matter how much humanity might express its views or actions, it cannot diminish the inherent majesty of God. God transcends all creation, and indeed, creation itself lacks meaning or value apart from God. In Psalm 113:4-6, it is written, *"The Lord is high above all nations, and his glory above the heavens! Who is like the Lord our God, who is seated on high, who looks far down on the heavens and the earth?"* This passage asserts that God's grandeur remains unaffected by human perceptions or actions.

The essence of divine majesty is not subject to human influence. St. Augustine of Hippo reflects on this in his *Confessions* 1.1, stating, *"You are great, Lord, and greatly to be praised; great is your power, and your wisdom is infinite"*. Augustine emphasizes that God's greatness is beyond human diminishment, emphasizing the eternal and unchanging nature of God's majesty.

On the other hand, an excessive focus on God's boundless mercy without recognizing the balance of His majesty may lead to imprudent interpretations. It is crucial to understand that God's nature encompasses both divine love and supreme authority. Romans 11:22 captures this balance, *"Note then the kindness and the severity of God: severity toward those who have fallen, but God's kindness to you, provided you continue in his kindness."* This verse highlights that divine love does not exclude divine authority and judgment but integrates both aspects into God's nature.

The concern here is that an emphasis on God's omnipotence and detachment from human affairs might lead to a perception that God created humanity and then withdrew. This view could imply a lack of on-going divine involvement in human life. However, Scripture presents an active, on-going relationship between God and humanity. Acts 17:27 affirms, *"He is actually not far from each one of us."* This verse emphasizes that God's presence remains intimately involved in human affairs.

Instead of merely exchanging criticisms, it is more productive to focus on points of agreement. The key issue is understanding the nature of the divine-human relationship. If one posits that God is fundamentally distant due to an absolute contrast with humanity, it challenges the very notion of an interactive relationship. Such an extreme dichotomy could negate the possibility of genuine interaction between the divine and the human.

Human experience reveals instances where opposites can interact under specific conditions, such as a common interest or a willingness to end conflict. Similarly, despite the absolute contrast between Creator and creation, a meaningful relationship is conceivable because humanity relies entirely on God.

The very nature of being a created being places humanity in a position where interaction with God is not only possible but necessary for understanding and faith. This highlights the centrality of divine-human interaction in understanding God's purpose.

This leads to a broader discussion on the nature of divine commands and the image of God they reflect. The traditional depiction of God issuing commands from a position of authority can be seen as a metaphor derived from political and social hierarchies, where a ruler issues orders to subjects. This view reflects a human-centric perspective of governance and power. For instance, Psalm 47:8

states, *"God reigns over the nations; God sits on his holy throne,"* using royal imagery to convey God's authority.

Conversely, an image of God characterized by unbounded compassion that eliminates all barriers might also stem from human desires for equality and freedom, projecting an idealized vision of divine interaction. Such a vision could be influenced by human experiences of deprivation and longing for an ideal state of being. The New Testament presents Jesus' teachings on love and compassion, emphasizing that *"God is love"* (1 John.4:8). This highlights a relational aspect of divine interaction, suggesting that God's nature includes a profound compassion that connects with human experience.

The critique here is that traditional views of God as an authoritarian figure reinforce notions of oppression, while more egalitarian depictions might better align with human aspirations for freedom. Each perspective carries its own risks and implications. For example, St. John Chrysostom, in his *Homilies on the Gospel of Matthew* 1, reflects on the nature of divine authority and compassion, emphasizing that God's commands are given with deep love and concern for human well-being.
To refine our understanding of divine nature and the relationship with humanity, it is essential to address these images critically. This involves relying on divine revelation as a foundational source for understanding.

2 Timothy 3:16 states, *"All Scripture is breathed out by God and profitable for teaching, for reproof, for correction, and for training in righteousness,"* underscoring the importance of Scripture in guiding understanding of divine nature. Additionally, employing rigorous intellectual analysis to examine prevailing ideas, their origins, and their impacts is

crucial in balancing reverence for divine majesty with an appreciation of divine love.

By critically engaging with these perspectives, one can strive for a more nuanced and accurate comprehension of the divine-human relationship, recognizing both the majesty and the love inherent in the divine nature.

The Nature of the Divine-Human Relationship: Contrasts and Similarities

The relationship between God and humanity, as understood within Christian theology, often grapples with the tension between perceived contradictions and recognized similarities. This relationship can be seen from different perspectives: whether it is fundamentally defined by inherent contradictions or whether common ground can be found. The crux of the issue is whether understanding God requires acknowledging contradictions or whether it can be based on recognizing commonalities between the divine and human experiences.

The idea of contradiction suggests that the divine and human natures are so fundamentally different that their interaction could only be theoretical or abstract. On one side, the relationship between God and humanity might be perceived through the lens of absolute difference, where God's transcendence and humanity's finitude create an insurmountable chasm. This perspective echoes the ancient philosophical concerns about the nature of divine immanence and transcendence. The Apostle Paul in his letters acknowledges this tension but also emphasizes the possibility of reconciliation through Christ. For instance, in Colossians 1:16-17, Paul writes, *"For by him all things were created, in heaven and on earth, visible and invisible... and in him all things hold together."*

This verse underscores the idea that despite the inherent differences between the Creator and the created, a unifying force exists in Christ.
Conversely, another view argues that while there are undeniable differences, recognizing some level of similarity between God and humanity is crucial for understanding their relationship. This notion suggests that divine revelation and the human experience are not entirely disparate but can interact in meaningful ways. The concept of divine revelation is central to this understanding. Revelation, according to Christian tradition, is not merely an abstract communication but a means of bridging the gap between the divine and human realms.

As stated in Hebrews 1:1-2, *"In the past God spoke to our ancestors through the prophets at many times and in various ways, but in these last days he has spoken to us by his Son."* This passage highlights the idea that divine revelation through Christ provides a means for God to engage directly with humanity.

The role of divine revelation in shaping the relationship between God and humanity cannot be underestimated. However, the critique that focusing solely on revelation might imply a fundamental contradiction between God and humanity is significant. If divine revelation were the only means of connecting with God, it might suggest a persistent divide between the two. This notion is challenged by the theological perspective that divine revelation is intended to foster a transformative relationship rather than simply convey information. As St. Augustine argues, *"For the reason that you understand and perceive that you are understanding and perceiving, is that you are not understanding and perceiving in a single moment, but that you are understanding and perceiving the things that are past or present or future"* (*Confessions*.10.8). Augustine's view emphasizes that understanding God involves more than just theoretical knowledge; it requires an experiential and transformative relationship.

The idea that contradictions might define the divine-human relationship raises questions about the nature of this interaction.

If God is wholly transcendent and humanity is inherently flawed, the connection between them might seem inherently flawed or unattainable. This perspective is countered by the belief that God's incarnation in Christ was a means of bridging this divide. The incarnation represents a profound union of divine and human natures, suggesting that the relationship between God and humanity is not defined by contradiction but by a transformative engagement.

Moreover, the goal of recovering a true sense of humanity and experiencing life in its fullness is crucial. This recovery involves a deeper understanding of God that transcends mere theoretical knowledge. It implies a genuine, transformative relationship that integrates with human existence.

The argument that God exists beyond human sensory perception and intellectual comprehension further complicates the discussion. Treating God as a subject of empirical study might seem inappropriate because it could reduce the divine to something material and finite. This view is supported by St. John Chrysostom, who notes, *"The divine nature is beyond our grasp and cannot be comprehended by the senses, but is known through its works"* (*Homilies on the Gospel of John* 8). Chrysostom's observation highlights that while human experience is limited, the divine can still be known through its manifestations and actions rather than direct sensory perception.

In conclusion, understanding the relationship between God and humanity involves navigating the tension between acknowledging profound differences and recognizing meaningful connections. Divine revelation plays a crucial role, but it should lead to a transformative understanding that integrates with human experience. This balance requires acknowledging that while God transcends human limitations, the relationship is designed to be deeply engaging and transformative, bridging the gap between divine majesty and human existence.

Part Two
The Incarnation:
Understanding Divine Union, Son-ship, and the Church

This part, titled "*The Incarnation: Understanding Divine Union, Son -ship, and the Church*," explores the multifaceted implications of the Incarnation for our understanding of divine union, the concept of son-ship, and the nature of the Church.

We begin with "*The Reasons for Incarnation*," a section that examines the theological and salvific motivations behind God's decision to become incarnate. This exploration highlights how the Incarnation is not a mere historical event but a purposeful act of divine love and redemption, providing the foundation for the subsequent discussions in this part.

In "*The Gift of Son-ship through the Incarnation of the Son*," we explore how the Incarnation extends the gift of divine son-ship to humanity. This segment reveals how through Christ's incarnation, human beings are invited into a new relationship with God, characterized by adoption and intimacy as sons and daughters of the Father.

"*The Means of Approaching the Incarnate God*" addresses how the Incarnation provides a tangible and accessible means for humanity to approach and engage with the divine. This discussion underscores the significance of Christ's human form as a bridge between the finite and the infinite, making the divine presence approachable and relatable.

The part then delves into "*The Complexity of Divine Relationship and Prayer*," analysing how the Incarnation influences our understanding of the relationship between humanity and God, particularly through the practice of prayer. This section explores the ways in which the Incarnation enriches and complicates our interaction with the divine.

Following this, "*The Meaning of Prayer in the Name of the Son*" investigates the significance of praying in Jesus' name. This discussion illuminates how the Incarnation affects our prayer life, offering a framework for understanding the power and purpose of invoking Christ in our spiritual communication with God.

"*The Transformation of Humanity's Relationship with God Due to the Incarnation*" focuses on how the Incarnation fundamentally alters the nature of human-divine interaction. This segment provides insights into the transformative impact of Christ's coming on our relationship with God, reshaping our spiritual identity and connection.

In "*The Eternal Nature of the Incarnation*," we explore the theological assertion that the Incarnation is not a transient event but an eternal reality. This section examines how the union of divinity and humanity in Christ continues to have implications for eternity.

"*Participation in the Divine Nature*" discusses the concept of believers sharing in the divine nature through their union with Christ. This segment highlights how the Incarnation enables humanity to partake in the divine life, transforming believers into partakers of God's own nature.

"*Like Christ in His Humanity*" reflects on the call for believers to emulate Christ's humanity. This discussion emphasizes the importance of modelling our lives after Christ's example, showcasing how His human experience serves as a paradigm for our own spiritual journey.

The part further explores "*The Union of Divinity and Humanity,*" a deep dive into the theological mystery of how divine and human natures coexist in the person of Christ. This exploration offers a nuanced understanding of the interplay between the infinite and the finite within the person of Jesus.

"*The Church as the Body of Christ*" examines the ecclesiological implications of the Incarnation, focusing on how the Church is conceived as the body of Christ. This section highlights the communal aspect of the Incarnation, revealing how believers are united in Christ as His living body on earth.

Finally, "*The Incarnation as the Basis for the Church's Formation*" discusses how the sacrament of the Eucharist plays a crucial role in the formation and sustenance of the Church. This segment underscores the Eucharist as a means of participating in the life of Christ and reinforcing the unity of the Church.

Through this part, we seek to offer a comprehensive understanding of the Incarnation, exploring its profound implications for divine union, son-ship, and the nature of the Church. By delving into these themes, we aim to deepen our grasp of how the Incarnation shapes our relationship with God, transforms our spiritual life, and binds us together as the body of Christ.

The Reasons for Incarnation

The incarnation is deeply rooted in understanding the nature of God and creation. The first aspect to consider is the nature of God, which is fundamentally distinct from that of created beings. The most significant difference lies in the fact that God is the Creator, and as such, He is the source of all existence and the wellspring of life. This distinction is paramount in Christian theology, where God is seen as the ultimate origin of everything that exists.

When we speak of God as the "*source*," we imply that there is no other cause or reason for the existence of beings except God. He is the Creator who designed and brought existence into being. This idea is well articulated in the Book of Genesis, where it is written, *"In the beginning God created the heavens and the earth"* (Gen. 1:1). This foundational verse establishes that the universe's existence is entirely dependent on God's will. Ancient religious thought often viewed God as the primal essence from which all creation emerged, a concept that resonated with the notion that God is the fundamental reality from which everything else derives. Early theologians like Irenaeus of Lyons argued this perspective, writing in *Against Heresies* 2.10 that *"God created the world out of nothing, and by His own will"*

However, the idea of creation from nothing, or *creation ex nihilo*, has become a cornerstone of Christian doctrine. This view emphasizes that God created the universe not from pre-existing materials but from nothing, underscoring His immense generosity and sovereignty. This doctrine is supported by various Biblical passages and theological reflections. For instance, in Hebrews 11:3, it is stated, *"By faith we understand that the universe was formed at God's command, so that what is seen was not made out of what was visible."* This verse reinforces the concept that creation was an act of divine will rather than a transformation of pre-existing matter.

The Greek philosophical view, which posited that matter is eternal and that God is more a craftsman than a Creator, contrasts sharply with the Christian belief in creation ex nihilo. According to this perspective, God was seen as shaping existing matter rather than creating it from nothing. This idea is considered inadequate within Christian theology, which maintains that all creatures are entirely dependent on God for their existence. This view of creation underscores the belief that God is the sole source of existence and life.

Religious perspectives on creation vary, and two main views are often discussed:

1. The first perspective suggests that God created the world, set it in motion according to natural laws, and then allowed it to operate independently. This view implies that the universe functions as a self-sustaining entity with inherent order, requiring no further divine intervention.

2. The second perspective posits that while natural laws exist, God continuously oversees and sustains the universe, perpetually creating life and maintaining it. This on-going act of creation signifies a divine generosity that is unceasing.

Christianity adheres to the second view, which is affirmed by various scriptural references. For example, John. 5:17 records Jesus saying, *"My Father is working until now, and I am working."*

This statement highlights the continuous nature of God's creative activity, suggesting that the divine work of sustaining and renewing creation is an ongoing process. This view contrasts with deistic perspectives, which often align more closely with Platonic ideas, suggesting that after initiating creation, God does not further intervene, leaving the universe to operate by its own laws.

The purpose behind the creation of the world is intimately connected to humanity's understanding of God. According to Christian doctrine, the ultimate goal of creation is to facilitate human knowledge of God, which is seen as the highest aspiration for humanity. Romans 11:36 articulates this purpose: *"For from him and through him and to him are all things. To him be glory forever. Amen."* This verse emphasizes that all creation is oriented towards understanding and glorifying God.

God's creation of humanity reflects His boundless love and is designed to instil in people a natural longing to know Him. This yearning reveals that humans recognize a profound mystery beyond their grasp, with God being that ultimate mystery. Augustine of Hippo, an early Church Father, echoed this sentiment in his *Confessions 1.1* where he writes, *"Our hearts are restless until they rest in You"*. This longing signifies an inherent awareness of a divine presence and an inherent desire to connect with God.

The concept of divine son-ship is a key element in understanding the relationship between God and humanity. This idea is not merely a product of human imagination but is grounded in what God endowed humanity with at creation and in the nature of God Himself. John 1:12 provides a scriptural basis for this idea: *"But to all who did receive him, who believed in his name, he gave the right to become children of God."* This verse reflects the transformative relationship where humanity is invited to become children of

God, signifying a profound and intimate connection with the divine.

This statement encapsulates the idea that God's incarnation was intended to elevate humanity to a new state of divine son-ship, reflecting God's infinite generosity and the transformative potential of this relationship. In summary, the concept of incarnation and creation ex nihilo highlights the profound relationship between God and humanity. It underscores the idea that God is the source of all existence and that His creative work is on-going and generous. Understanding these theological principles is crucial for grasping the nature of God's interaction with creation and humanity. The relationship between God and humanity is characterized by a continuous and transformative divine engagement, reflecting both the majesty and the boundless love of God.

The Gift of Son-ship through the Incarnation of the Son

The notion of humanity being granted the status of God's children from the moment of creation is a profound theological concept. This idea is rooted in the understanding that humans were created in the "*image of God*," which implies that they were endowed with the potential for divine son-ship. This potential was realized through the incarnation, where God, through the Son, united with human nature to restore what was lost due to the separation from its divine origin.

The concept that humans are made in the "*image of God*" is first articulated in Genesis 1:26-27: "*Then God said, 'Let us make mankind in our image, in our likeness...' So God created mankind in his own image, in the image of God he created them; male and female he created them."* This foundational text signifies that humanity was created with a unique potential to reflect the divine nature, establishing a basis for a relationship akin to divine son-ship.

The incarnation is central to Christian theology as it represents the moment when God united with human nature in the person of Jesus Christ. John 1:14 underscores this transformative event: *"The Word became flesh and made his dwelling among us."* This verse highlights the union of divinity with humanity, a crucial aspect of restoring the relationship between God and humanity that was fractured by sin and separation from the divine source.

The question arises whether the incarnation was the only means to remedy humanity's estrangement from God. Although God, having created humanity from nothing, could theoretically restore the relationship with a mere command, the nature of the resolution requires more than mere divine power. The restoration of the relationship between God and humanity cannot be achieved by unilateral divine action alone. It requires a mutual engagement, involving human awareness, will, and choice. Saint Athanasius, in his work *On the Incarnation* (1:2), elaborates on this by stating that the incarnation was necessary not only to exercise divine power but to engage human freedom and choice in the process of restoration.

The divine approach to resolving humanity's estrangement involved not only power but also love. This aspect is critical because the divine resolution aimed to entice human acceptance rather than impose it through sheer power. Divine love, characterized by patience and persistent effort, is different from force. As Saint Irenaeus of Lyons writes in Against Heresies 3.18, God's love is expressed through a continuous and patient effort to restore humanity without coercion, highlighting the importance of a free and willing response to the divine invitation.

In this context, the idea of "*infusion*" or "*new infusion*" refers to the union of divinity with humanity in Christ, which endowed human nature with a new vitality impervious to decay and death. Saint Cyril of Alexandria, in *The Incarnation of the Word* 9, explains, "*By taking our nature upon Himself, He restored it and granted it a new, incorruptible life.*" This infusion is a significant aspect of the incarnation, providing humanity with the means to overcome mortality and corruption.

The human condition, subject to death and corruption, required an approach from the source of life itself. The incarnation served as a bridge between God and humanity, allowing divine life to be imparted to humanity.

This concept is reinforced by Gregory of Nazianzus in *Theological Orations* 5:10, who states, "*The Son of God assumed our nature, so that by uniting it with His own, He might bestow on it a new, eternal life.*" This union is essential for overcoming the limitations imposed by human mortality.

The idea that God chose the incarnation over mere divine command reflects a deeper understanding of the nature of divine-human interaction. The solution to the estrangement was not just a matter of exercising divine power but involved a relational and transformative process. The incarnation was not only a corrective measure but also a means of elevating human nature and restoring it to its intended divine potential.

In summary, the concept of the incarnation is intricately tied to the restoration of humanity's divine potential. By becoming incarnate, God provided humanity with a means to overcome death and corruption, infusing human nature with divine life. This profound event signifies more than a mere restoration of the divine-human relationship; it represents the elevation of human nature to its original divine potential, facilitated through a transformative union of divinity and humanity. This understanding reflects the depth and significance of the incarnation in Christian theology, emphasizing the role of divine love and human freedom in the process of restoration.

The Means of Approaching the Incarnate God

The idea that human beings, created in the "*image of God*," were endowed with the potential to attain divine son-ship. This potential is actualized in the figure of Christ, who is understood as the "*second Adam*," a new head of humanity analogous to the first Adam. Just as Adam was the progenitor of the old humanity, Christ, as the new Adam, is the source of a new, transformative humanity, which has an authentic and transformative relationship with God, distinct from the old, fallen state.

The term "*born from Christ*" reflects the belief that this new nature is directly derived from Him. This is a miraculous birth that transcends natural laws, paralleling Christ's own miraculous birth from the Virgin Mary through the Holy Spirit. The apostle John emphasizes this in John 1:12-13: "*But to all who did receive him, who believed in his name, he gave the right to become children of God, who were born, not of blood nor of the will of the flesh nor of the will of man, but of God.*" This rebirth represents a new divine origin, aligning believers with Christ's own divine nature.

While the original creation of humanity was an act of divine power, the rebirth through baptism involves the power of the Holy Spirit. As noted in John 3:5-6, Jesus explains to Nicodemus: "*Very truly I tell you, no one can enter the kingdom of God unless they are born of water and the Spirit. Flesh gives birth to flesh, but the Spirit gives birth to spirit."* This highlights the Holy Spirit's role in the process of spiritual rebirth.

This underscores that Christ's incarnation and subsequent work are pivotal for imparting divine son-ship to humanity. Athanasius argues that the incarnation is essential for humanity's restoration, as it bridges the divide created by sin and death.

The Holy Spirit plays a crucial role in this process, conveying divine son-ship from Christ to believers. As described in John 16:14, Christ says: *"He will glorify me because it is from me that he will receive what he will make known to you."* This passage illustrates the Spirit's function in transmitting Christ's divine nature to believers, enabling them to partake in the divine son-ship.

Furthermore, the sacrament of baptism symbolizes participation in Christ's death and resurrection. As Paul writes in Romans 6:4: *"We were therefore buried with him through baptism into death in order that, just as Christ was raised from the dead through the glory of the Father, we too may live a new life."* Through baptism, believers undergo a transformation, crucifying their old, sinful nature and receiving a new nature aligned with Christ's divine life.

This transformation is further elucidated by early Church Fathers. Irenaeus of Lyons, in *Against Heresies* 5.16, articulates: *"The Word, by becoming what we are, might bring us to be even what He is Himself"*. This statement reflects the profound impact of the incarnation, which bridges the gap between humanity and divinity and enables believers to participate in divine life.

The role of Christ as both the incarnate Son and the pre-incarnate Word is integral to understanding His dual nature and mission. Christ's dual role does not entail a contradiction but reveals different aspects of His nature. As the Son of God, Christ maintains His divine son-ship while also serving as the mediator and saviour for humanity. This duality is essential for comprehending how Christ interacts with both God and humanity, reflecting His unique nature and mission.

The Church Fathers provide further insight into this dual role. Saint Cyril of Alexandria, in his *Commentary on the Gospel of John*.1 writes: *"Christ is both Son of God and Son of Man; He is one person, the same in both natures, but He reveals the two natures distinctly"*. This distinction underscores Christ's role in addressing both the divine and human dimensions of His mission.

In summary, the idea of humanity's divine son-ship and the transformative power of Christ's incarnation are central to Christian theology. The interplay between divine son-ship, the role of the Holy Spirit, and the sacrament of baptism highlights the profound nature of Christ's work in restoring humanity's relationship with God. Through the teachings of early Church Fathers and scriptural revelations, this understanding is deepened, offering a comprehensive view of the divine-human relationship and the transformative impact of Christ's incarnation.

The Complexity of Divine Relationship and Prayer

The relationship between humanity and God is inherently complex, reflecting the depth and seriousness of such an engagement. Relationships, whether personal or divine, are seldom simple, particularly when they are genuine and meaningful. For instance, prior to marriage, a relationship might appear straightforward and romantic, but once it deepens through marriage, it inevitably becomes more intricate and challenging. Similarly, our relationship with God, who is present in every moment and every place, cannot be expected to be simpler than our relationships with friends and acquaintances.

The complexity arises not from God's actions, as God does not create problems for humans, but from the nature of God, which is fundamentally different from that of humans. This disparity requires heightened awareness and a deeper connection. When a person prays, they are engaging with the Creator in a way that goes beyond mere human interaction. It is not a matter of deceiving or simplifying the interaction but recognizing the profound nature of this relationship.

The incarnation of God in Christ does not imply a loss of divinity or a simplification of God's nature. Even with Christ's embodiment, God did not cease to be omnipresent. This means that when praying, believers address God through the mediation of Christ, who participated in human nature while remaining divine. Thus, prayers are made in Christ's name, reflecting the profound truth that Christ, as part of humanity, is the intermediary who has bridged the divine and human realms. As St. Athanasius asserts in *On the Incarnation* 4, *"Christ did not diminish His divine nature by assuming our human condition; rather, He unified our nature with the divine in a way that transcends all human comprehension."*

Understanding this relationship requires acknowledging that the divine essence of God is not confined to the physical body of Christ. The human body, while the manifestation of Christ's divine love and care, does not restrict His divine nature.

Hence, when praying to the incarnate God, it is crucial not to envision the divine essence as limited to the physical form of Christ, as this concept contradicts the infinite nature of God. St. Gregory of Nyssa elucidates this point in *Against Eunomius* 1.6 , saying, *"The divine nature of Christ is not confined to His physical appearance; rather, He remains omnipresent and immutable, even as He has taken on the form of a servant."*

In prayer, the believer approaches the divine in the name of Christ, and this act is not limited by Christ's earthly presence. The divine presence remains fully intact in heaven. The Trinity — Father, Son, and Holy Spirit — shares a single divine essence, will, and purpose. This unity means that praying to the Father is also acknowledging the Son and the Holy Spirit. St. Cyril of Alexandria, in *Commentary on John* 3.14, writes, *"The three Persons of the Holy Trinity act in perfect unity and harmony. When we address the Father in our prayers, we do so in the presence and with the acknowledgment of the Son and the Holy Spirit."*

This understanding clarifies that the divine nature of God encompasses all aspects of the Trinity, and that prayers, while made in Christ's name, are also a recognition of the unity and presence of the Father and the Holy Spirit. The complexity of this relationship does not diminish its depth but rather highlights the multifaceted nature of divine interaction and the profoundness of prayer. St. Augustine, in his *Confessions* 10.6, states, *"In every prayer, we engage with the full mystery of the Trinity. Although we speak to the Father, we do so in the name of the Son and through the mediation of the Holy Spirit, acknowledging the inseparable unity of the divine essence."*

Thus, the intricate nature of divine-human interaction reflects a profound truth about the nature of God and the relational dynamics established through the incarnation. As believers approach God through prayer, they participate in a relationship that encompasses the entirety of the divine essence and acknowledges the unity and distinct roles of the Trinity. This depth and complexity underscore the significance of understanding and engaging with God in a manner that respects the full breadth of His divine nature.

The Meaning of Prayer in the Name of the Son

The praying in the name of the Son is deeply significant and intricately connected to the relationship between humanity and God, particularly after the Incarnation. This relationship, established through the Son, is not merely about invoking a name but understanding the profound privileges and benefits it entails. When believers pray to the Father, they do so by invoking the name of the Son, expressing gratitude for the extraordinary gifts received—gifts that include the honour of being called His children, a privilege made possible only through the Son.

In John 14:13-14, Jesus assures His followers, *"Whatever you ask in my name, this I will do, that the Father may be glorified in the Son. If you ask me anything in my name, I will do it."* This passage underscores the transformative power inherent in praying in Jesus' name. According to St. John Chrysostom in his *Homily 82 on the Gospel of John,* *"Christ is the mediator between God and humanity;*

through Him, our prayers are sanctified and brought to the Father". Chrysostom highlights that Christ, as mediator, bridges the gap between the divine and human realms, facilitating a more profound connection with God through prayer.

This mediation role signifies that Christ does not merely represent believers but actively participates in presenting their prayers to the Father. St. Augustine, in *On the Trinity* 5.10.15, provides further insight into this concept : *"The name of the Son is a powerful conduit to the Father, for it signifies the profound unity and love between the Father and the Son"*. Augustine emphasizes that invoking the name of the Son in prayer acknowledges the deep unity between Christ and the Father, affirming that the Son's authority and presence play a crucial role in the efficacy of prayer.

The nature of prayer, when viewed through the lens of relationships, becomes even more significant. Although the specific term *"relationship"* might not be frequently used in the New Testament, the essence of spiritual engagement is relational.

For instance, in John 15:15, Jesus states, *"No longer do I call you servants, for the servant does not know what his master is doing; but I have called you friends, for all that I have heard from my Father I have made known to you."* This declaration reflects a profound shift from servitude to intimate friendship, highlighting the depth of the connection that Christ seeks to establish with His followers.

St. Irenaeus, in *Against Heresies*5.36 observes, *"The relationship between God and humanity is dynamic and evolving, for God imparts His grace to continually uplift and transform His creation"*. Irenaeus underscores that the divine-human relationship is not static but is characterized by on-going growth and transformation. God's grace facilitates this dynamic process, allowing believers to partake in the divine nature and progress in their spiritual journey.

In praying in the name of the Son, believers acknowledge that this relationship is not confined to earthly terms but is deeply rooted in the divine economy. This understanding is reflected in 2 Peter 1:4, which states, *"He has granted to us his precious and very great promises, so that through them you may become partakers of the divine nature."* This verse illustrates that the relationship with God is continuously developing as believers grow into their divine calling. The promises of God are the means through which believers are integrated into the divine life, demonstrating that the divine-human relationship involves on-going transformation and spiritual growth.

The dynamic nature of this relationship is further explored by St. Athanasius in *On the Incarnation* 54, where he writes, *"The Incarnation of the Son was not only for the sake of redemption but also to restore and elevate human nature, so that through the Son, humanity might be renewed and participate in the divine nature"*. Athanasius highlights that the Incarnation serves both a redemptive and transformative purpose, emphasizing the profound impact of Christ's role in bridging the gap between God and humanity.

In summary, the concept of praying in the name of the Son reflects a profound understanding of the divine-human relationship.

This relationship, deeply rooted in the privileges of divine son-ship and friendship, is dynamic and evolving. Through Christ's mediation, believers gain access to the Father and participate in the divine nature, showcasing the on-going transformation and spiritual growth inherent in this sacred connection. The teachings of Scripture and the early Church Fathers collectively emphasize the depth and significance of this relationship, underscoring the importance of understanding prayer as an expression of the profound unity and on-going interaction between God and humanity.

The Transformation of Humanity's Relationship with God Due to the Incarnation

The Incarnation significantly altered the relationship between humanity and God, introducing profound changes that reshaped the understanding of human destiny and divine interaction. Before the Incarnation, humanity's relationship with God was characterized by a sense of distance and anticipation. The Old Testament provides a framework within which this relationship was mediated through laws, rituals, and prophecies. The divine-human interaction was indirect and often shrouded in mystery, reflecting the partial understanding of God's plans for humanity.

In the Old Testament, God's covenant with Israel, while central, emphasized the distance between the divine and human realms. For instance, in Leviticus 26:12, God promises, "*I will walk among you and be your God, and you shall be my people.*" This promise, though intimate, was mediated through laws and rituals that underscored the separation between the divine and the human. The Law was a guide but also a barrier, reflecting the limitations of human understanding and access to God's full presence.

The Incarnation brought a radical shift in this relationship by directly uniting divinity with humanity in the person of Jesus Christ. This union provided a new level of intimacy and clarity. As stated in John 1:14, "*And the Word became flesh and dwelt among us, and we have seen his glory, glory as of the only Son from the Father, full of grace and truth."* This verse highlights the transition from a mediated relationship to a direct encounter with the divine, where God's nature and intentions are fully revealed.

This statement reflects the profound impact of the Incarnation on human destiny. By becoming human, the Son of God made it possible for humanity to share in divine grace and eternal life, revealing a clear and eternal destiny that was previously obscured.

The Incarnation also shifted humanity's status from being distant to being intimately connected with God. This union was not merely symbolic but transformative, as the divine presence became accessible through Christ. Saint Cyril of Alexandria in his *Commentary on the Gospel of John* 4.14 emphasizes the significance of this union: *"The Word became flesh to elevate humanity to participate in the divine nature"*. This participation in the divine nature does not mean that humanity becomes divine in essence but rather shares in the divine grace and life that Christ imparts.

It is crucial to understand that while humanity benefits from this union, it does not imply becoming divine in the same way Christ is divine. The early Church Fathers were careful to distinguish between participation in divine grace and the notion of deification. Saint Peter, in 2 Peter 1:4, writes, *"By which he has granted to us his precious and very great promises, so that through them you may become partakers of the divine nature, having escaped from the corruption that is in the world because of sinful desire."* This participation is about sharing in divine attributes and grace without altering the fundamental nature of humanity.

Saint Athanasius further clarifies this distinction in *On the Incarnation* 7, *"The Word was made flesh to renew our nature, but this renewal does not imply that our nature becomes divine"*.

This perspective is critical to understanding the nature of human transformation through the Incarnation. The renewal provided by Christ elevates humanity to a new level of grace and relationship with God while preserving human nature's distinctiveness.

Saint Cyril of Alexandria, in *Commentary on the Gospel of John* 4.14, reiterates the careful balance between divinity and humanity: *"The union of the divine and human natures in Christ signifies a real and transformative interaction, but it does not suggest that human nature itself is transformed into divinity"*. This understanding underscores the on-going partnership between God and humanity established through the Incarnation, highlighting the transformative yet preserving impact of this divine-human union.

In summary, the Incarnation introduced a new clarity to the relationship between humanity and God, transforming human destiny and status while allowing for a profound participation in divine grace. The teachings of the early Church Fathers and the biblical texts provide a nuanced understanding of this transformation, emphasizing the intimate and transformative nature of the divine-human relationship while preserving the integrity of human nature.

The Eternal Nature of the Incarnation

The concept of the eternal nature of the Incarnation signifies that the humanity assumed by the Lord will endure forever. This profound reality is a cornerstone of Christian theology, reflecting the deep and unending bond between the divine and human natures of Christ. This union of Christ's divine and human natures is not transient but eternal, ensuring that the Son who assumed human flesh remains forever united with humanity.

This understanding aligns with the teachings of the New Testament. In Ephesians 1:22-23, Paul declares, *"And He put all things under His feet and gave Him as head over all things to the church, which is His body, the fullness of Him who fills all in all."* This passage emphasizes that Christ's role as the head of the Church is everlasting, reflecting the eternal nature of the Incarnation. Similarly, in 1 Corinthians 15:28, Paul writes, *"When all things are subjected to Him, then the Son Himself will also be subjected to Him who put all things under Him, that God may be all in all."* This indicates that after the final judgment, believers will experience an eternal union with the divine, where God will be the all-encompassing reality for those who are saved.

The transformation that believers will undergo, receiving glorified bodies akin to Christ's own resurrected body, is a significant aspect of this eternal union. Philippians 3:21 promises, *"Who will transform our lowly body that it may be conformed to His glorious body."* This transformation involves more than just a physical change; it reflects a deep participation in the divine nature. The radiance of Christ during the Transfiguration, described in Matthew 17:2, *"His face shone like the sun,"* offers a foretaste of the divine glory that believers will share. This glory, however, is not a result of independent action but is given as a gift through Christ's union with the divine.

The New Testament also suggests that in the age to come, there will be no need for miracles such as healing, as all bodily imperfections will be removed. In 1 Corinthians 15:43, Paul notes, *"It is sown in dishonour; it is raised in glory,"* which signifies that the present mortal condition, marked by dishonour and decay, will be replaced by a glorified, immortal state. The miraculous works performed by Christ were meant to reveal His divine authority and compassion but are not the ultimate goal. The absence of miracles in the resurrected state underscores the completeness of divine restoration and healing.

Christ's statement in John 14:12, *"The works that I do shall you do also; and greater works than these shall you do,"* is often interpreted within the context of Christ's will and purpose. The miracles performed by Christ were not automatic but were dependent on His divine will.

The story of the woman with the issue of blood, who was healed among many who touched Jesus (Mark. 5:25-34), illustrates that miracles occur through Christ's purposeful intervention rather than by mere physical contact. Even Judas Iscariot, despite his close association with Jesus, did not benefit from this healing power, further emphasizing that miracles are not a product of proximity but of divine will.

Participation in the Divine Nature

The participating in the divine nature is central to understanding the implications of the Incarnation. This idea was a major point of contention in early Church debates, particularly against Arianism, which denied the full divinity of Christ. Saint Athanasius, in *On the Incarnation* 54, contended that if Christ were not truly divine, believers could not share in the divine nature. The notion of deification or the elevation of human nature through union with Christ does not imply that humans become divine by essence but that they share in the divine life through Christ.

The Bible teaches that immortality is a gift from God rather than an inherent human attribute. Romans 6:23 asserts, *"The wages of sin is death, but the gift of God is eternal life in Christ Jesus our Lord,"* indicating that immortality is bestowed by divine grace. God is described as *"immortal, dwelling in unapproachable light"* in 1Timothy 6:16, affirming that immortality is a divine characteristic. The hymn *"Holy God, Holy Mighty, Holy Immortal"* reflects this understanding of God's eternal nature.

Human beings, being mortal and finite, can only receive immortality through communion with God. This aligns with the fall of Adam, who lost eternal life through separation from God (Gen. 3:22-24). Just as Adam's expulsion from Eden represents a loss of eternal life, so does separation from God lead to spiritual death. Conversely, communion with God, restored through Christ, grants eternal life.

The fate of the wicked is a challenging issue. While the specifics of eternal death are not exhaustively detailed in Scripture, the early Church Fathers maintained that the resurrection of the wicked would be a continuation of their separation from God.

This view is supported by the belief that the righteous will shine like the sun in the kingdom of their Father (Matt 13:43), while the wicked will face outer darkness, a metaphor for eternal separation from God (Matt.25:30). The transformation into a glorified state, as exemplified by Christ's resurrection, is reserved for the righteous.

In summary, the participation in the divine nature, as understood through the lens of the Incarnation, emphasizes that believers are granted a share in divine immortality through their union with Christ. This contrasts with the fate of those who remain outside this communion, highlighting the profound implications of the Incarnation for the divine-human relationship and the eternal destiny of believers. The early Church Fathers, particularly Athanasius, played a crucial role in articulating these doctrines, defending the reality of Christ's divinity and the transformative power of the Incarnation.

Like Christ in His Humanity

Becoming exactly like Christ, if understood as a complete and exact replication, is fundamentally flawed. Christ is the second Person of the Trinity, the only Son, and the Word of God who is the source of life. In contrast, human beings possess life only through Him. The notion of transforming ourselves to become exactly like Him is as implausible as a branch becoming a vine. As Jesus said, *"I am the vine; you are the branches"* (John.15:5). Without the vine, the branch withers and is cast into the fire, highlighting that human beings, apart from Christ, cannot achieve the divine status of the Son. This is consistent with John 15:6, where Christ underscores that *"If anyone does not abide in Me, he is cast out as a branch and is withered."*

The term *"participate"* in the context of the divine nature implies receiving and taking, acknowledging a lack or need. This is reflected in Christ's teaching to *"ask, and it will be given to you"* (Matt. 7:7), which points to the dependence of humanity on divine grace rather than independent possession.

Paul's metaphor of the Church as the body of Christ in 1 Corinthians 12:12-27 further illustrates this dependence: *"For as the body is one and has many members, but all the members of that one body, being many, are one body, so also is Christ."* Just as the body relies on every part to function, believers rely on Christ for spiritual sustenance.

The analogy of the canal drawing from a river conveys a profound truth: the divine life flowing through us is a reflection of God's eternal life. Ezekiel's vision of the river flowing from the temple (Ezek. 47:1-12) symbolizes this divine provision. The river, representing the Holy Spirit, sustains the canal, akin to how believers are sustained by God's grace. As Ezekiel describes, the river's water brings life and healing, underscoring the continuous and life-giving relationship believers maintain with God.

This participation includes receiving immortality and sonship, fundamental blessings from God. The concept of believers becoming co-heirs with Christ is supported by Paul's statement in Romans 8:17, *"And if children, then heirs—heirs of God and joint heirs with Christ."* The firstborn, according to Hebrew customs, inherits the blessings of the Father and has authority over his siblings.

Human beings have no inherent qualification for son-ship; it is solely a gift from God through Jesus Christ, His true and only Son. The Incarnation is pivotal in humanity's attainment of this honor. Before the Incarnation, the Son was eternally the Son of God. The Incarnation did not diminish this son-ship but revealed it. As Athanasius explains, *"The Word became flesh, and by this union, He brought humanity into a new relationship with God"* (*On the Incarnation*, 10). The union of divinity and humanity in Christ is a true and actual union, making the Incarnation the means through which this son-ship is proclaimed.

The eternal son-ship is beyond human comprehension, including the understanding of angels. The Incarnation's purpose was to reveal the Son's eternal son-ship to the Father. This is evident from the Gospel of Matthew, where Christ's baptism is accompanied by the Father's voice declaring, *"This is My beloved Son, in whom I am well pleased"*

(Matt.3:17). This affirmation at the Jordan River confirms the Son's unique divine relationship, underscoring the importance of the Incarnation in manifesting this divine son-ship.

Without Christ's humanity, discussions of His anointing would be meaningless. Christ's offering of His body to death and subsequent resurrection signifies that humanity has been rendered incorruptible. As Paul states, *"For the death that He died, He died to sin once for all; but the life that He lives, He lives to God"* (Rom. 6:10). The divine nature does not die, but humanity did die because it was mortal. After the resurrection, the union of divinity and humanity was complete, rendering humanity impervious to death. Paul writes, *"And declared to be the Son of God with power according to the Spirit of holiness, by the resurrection from the dead"* (Rom.1:4).

The Transfiguration and Christ's post-resurrection powers reveal the glory of the divine through humanity. After His resurrection, Christ ascended into heaven with His glorified body, making it visible to believers. Saint Cyril of Alexandria notes that *"The glory of Christ's divinity was revealed through His human flesh"* (*Commentary on the Gospel of John* 12. 3). The Incarnation made clear the nature of the Trinity and the divine glory of the Son, bestowing blessings upon humanity. The complete union of divinity with humanity through the resurrection means that before the resurrection, humanity was subject to mortality, suffering, and pain. After the resurrection, these weaknesses vanished, leaving humanity free from anything inconsistent with divine glory.

Saint Gregory of Nyssa elaborates that the resurrection and Transfiguration were not merely historical events but profound revelations of the divine nature integrated with humanity. He asserts,

"The divine nature did not change; it was manifested through the mortal flesh" (*Great Catechism* 26).

This integration ensures that divine glory, revealed through the risen Christ, encompasses the transformation of humanity into a state of glory and immortality, reflecting the full realization of the divine purpose.

In conclusion, the participation in the divine nature is foundational to understanding the divine-human relationship. It signifies that believers, through their union with Christ, are granted a share in divine immortality, contrasting sharply with the fate of those who remain outside this divine communion.

The Union of Divinity and Humanity

The concept of the complete union between divinity and humanity in the womb of the Virgin Mary is a profound aspect of Christian doctrine that has been discussed extensively by early Church Fathers and is rooted in biblical teachings. This union is central to understanding the nature of Christ and His role in salvation history.

St. Cyril of Alexandria provides a crucial explanation regarding this union. He elaborates that the phrase *"increasing in wisdom and stature and in favour with God and man"* (Luke.2:52) refers specifically to Christ's human nature. Cyril's commentary emphasizes that the Word of God, while remaining divine, allowed His humanity to develop according to human nature and laws. He intended that His divine glory be revealed progressively, so as not to overwhelm human perception. Cyril explains this gradual revelation of divine perfection in *Commentary on the Gospel of Luke* 2, 27. The wonder expressed by those who witnessed Jesus' wisdom, as recorded in John 7:15, *"How does this man know letters, having never been educated?"* reflects the divine wisdom manifested in a manner that was accessible to human understanding.

The resurrection of Christ also follows this pattern of gradual revelation, as it reflects the full glory of divinity revealed through humanity.

This is evident in passages like 1 Corinthians 15:20, where Paul states, *"But now Christ is risen from the dead, and has become the first fruits of those who have fallen asleep."* The resurrection, thus, is a key event that demonstrates the complete union of divine and human natures.

Understanding that the body of Christ was the means through which the Son of God, the Father, and the Holy Spirit were revealed is crucial. Galatians 4:4-5 states, *"But when the fullness of the time had come, God sent forth His Son, born of a woman, born under the law, to redeem those who were under the law, that we might receive the adoption as sons."* This verse indicates that the Incarnation was specifically an act of the Son, not the Father or the Holy Spirit. Despite this, the Son's earthly ministry also revealed the Father and the Holy Spirit.

Jesus' declaration in John 14:9, *"He who has seen Me has seen the Father,"* and John 10:30, *"I and the Father are one,"* highlights the unity between the Son and the Father. This unity is essential for understanding the revelation of divine attributes through Christ. The love and sacrifice of both the Father and the Son are manifested in Christ's death and resurrection, underscoring the shared divine purpose in salvation.

The Holy Spirit's role in this revelation is also significant. While the Spirit was present during Christ's baptism, descending *"like a dove"* (Matt. 3:16), His full manifestation awaited Pentecost. Acts 2:3 describes this as *"tongues of fire,"* which represented a visible sign of the Spirit's presence and power. St. Irenaeus, in his work *Against Heresies* 3. 16 ,notes that the Holy Spirit reveals the Son, and through the Son, the Father. This hierarchical revelation ensures that the human mind is not overwhelmed by the direct manifestation of the Spirit.

The Holy Spirit's role in revealing the Son, rather than Himself, is intentional to prevent confusion. Some Church Fathers, such as St. Augustine in *on Trinity* 1.2, suggest that the full revelation of the Holy Spirit will occur in the eschatological age. The *"hidden manna"* referred to in Revelation 2:17 symbolizes the Spirit as the source of divine sustenance and life in the heavenly Jerusalem. This imagery underscores the Spirit's indirect revelation through the Son.

The question of whether the Incarnation delayed the revelation of the Holy Spirit's person is significant. The Incarnation of the Son prepared the way for the Spirit's indirect revelation. The Holy Spirit's nature remains largely invisible, emphasizing that understanding the Spirit's role is facilitated through the visible Incarnation of the Son.

Regarding the descent of the Holy Spirit upon Christ at the Jordan River, it is important to understand that this event was related to Christ's human nature and not a division of the Son. The Gospels affirm that the Spirit's descent was a preparation for Christ's ministry, not a separation of His divine and human natures. The Fathers of the Church, including St. Athanasius in *On the Incarnation* 8, maintain that the Spirit's descent was for the benefit of humanity, aligning with Christ's mission as the second Adam.

The notion of dividing the Son into two entities due to the Spirit's descent is unfounded. The Gospels clearly describe the Spirit's descent as a preparation for Christ's divine mission (Luke 3:22). Paul's statement in Romans 8:11, *"But if the Spirit of Him who raised Jesus from the dead dwells in you, He who raised Christ from the dead will also give life to your mortal bodies through His Spirit who dwells in you,"* underscores the unity of Christ's divine and human natures. The resurrection of Christ, which was accomplished *"through the Spirit,"* confirms this unity.

The concern about whether the Incarnation divides the Son into two parts can be addressed by recognizing that Christ's human nature did not divide His divine nature. The experience of death and resurrection highlighted the unity of His person. As Paul states in Romans 6:10, *"For the death that He died, He died to sin once for all; but the life that He lives, He lives to God."* The resurrection transforms Christ's mortal body into an immortal one, affirming the unity of divinity and humanity. This transformation is a promise of eternal life to all who are united with Him, particularly through the Eucharist. Christ's assurance in John 6:40, *"I will raise him up at the last day,"* reflects this promise.

In summary, the union of divinity and humanity in Christ is a complex but central doctrine in Christianity. The teachings of the early Church Fathers, supported by scriptural references, provide a profound understanding of this union and its implications for salvation and eternal life. The Incarnation, as a manifestation of divine and human unity, reveals the nature of God and His plan for humanity, offering a promise of eternal communion with Him.

The Church as the Body of Christ

The deep understanding of the Church as the Body of Christ flows naturally from the doctrine of the Incarnation, which asserts that God became fully human in the person of Jesus Christ. The Apostle Paul is the primary advocate of the concept of the Church as the Body of Christ, particularly in his letters to the Corinthians, Ephesians, and Romans. In 1 Corinthians 12:12-27, Paul describes the Church as a body composed of many members, each with its unique function, yet all integral to the unity of the whole. He emphasizes that this unity is not based on external conformity but on the shared life of Christ that flows through each believer. Paul writes, *"For just as the body is one and has many members, and all the members of the body, though many, are one body, so it is with Christ"* (1 Cor.12:12). Paul further elaborates on this idea in Ephesians 4:15-16, where he describes the Church's growth and development, emphasizing the role of Christ as the head who directs and sustains the body. He writes, *"Rather, speaking the truth in love, we are to grow up in every way into him who is the head, into Christ, from whom the whole body, joined and held together by every joint with which it is equipped, when each part is working properly, makes the body grow so that it builds itself up in love"* (Eph.4:15-16). Here, Paul presents a vision of the Church as an interconnected, dynamic organism that is built up in love through the effective working of its diverse members.

The relationship between the Incarnation and the Church as the Body of Christ is profound and multifaceted. The Incarnation is the cornerstone of the Church's identity as Christ's body, ensuring that the Church is more than a mere human institution; it is the continuation of Christ's incarnational presence in the world. The Church, therefore, embodies the reality of the Incarnation, carrying forward the mission of Christ. Just as the Incarnation was God's definitive act of entering into human history, the Church is called to be the tangible expression of Christ's presence in the world today. The Church, as the Body of Christ, is entrusted with the mission of continuing Christ's work on earth—preaching the gospel, healing the sick, caring for the poor, and embodying God's love and justice. This idea is grounded in Jesus' own words to His disciples, as recorded in John 20:21: "*As the Father has sent me, even so I am sending you.*"

The Incarnation reveals the profound unity of divine and human natures in the person of Jesus Christ. This unity is mirrored in the Church, which, though composed of diverse members with different gifts, backgrounds, and roles, is united in Christ. Paul's metaphor of the body illustrates this unity in diversity, where each member, though distinct, contributes to the health and function of the whole. The Church's unity reflects the unity found in Christ, who embodies both the fullness of divinity and humanity.

The early Church Fathers recognized and expounded upon the deep connection between the Incarnation and the Church as the Body of Christ. St. Athanasius, in his seminal work *On the Incarnation*, famously stated, "*He became what we are so that we might become what He is*" (*On the Incarnation*, 54). This statement highlights the transformative aspect of the Incarnation, where Christ's taking on human nature enables humanity to partake in the divine nature. This transformative reality is lived out in the life of the Church, where believers are continually being conformed to the image of Christ. St. Augustine also contributed significantly to this understanding. In his writings, Augustine frequently referred to the Church as the "*whole Christ*" (*Christus totus*), encompassing both the head (*Christ*) and the body (*the Church*). He believed that through the communal life of the Church, believers are united to Christ and participate in His divine life. Augustine writes, "*For you are the body of Christ and His members. If, therefore, you are the body of Christ and His members, your mystery is placed on the Lord's table: you receive your mystery*" (*Sermon* 341). This reflects the profound unity between Christ and His Church, grounded in the Incarnation.

The Incarnation and the Church as the Body of Christ are deeply interconnected doctrines that shape the identity and mission of the Church. The Incarnation is the divine act that makes the Church's existence as Christ's body possible, ensuring that the Church is a continuation of Christ's presence in the world. Through its unity in diversity and its mission, the Church embodies the reality of the Incarnation, living out Christ's love and truth in every aspect of its communal and individual life. This understanding is rooted in the teachings of Scripture, particularly in the writings of Paul, and has been richly developed by the early Church Fathers, such as St. Athanasius and St. Augustine. Their insights continue to guide the Church in understanding its profound connection to Christ through the mystery of the Incarnation.

The Incarnation as the Basis for the Church's Formation

The Church, within the rich tapestry of Christian theology, is often adorned with vivid metaphors that illuminate its profound relationship with Christ and its indispensable role in the divine plan of salvation. Prominent among these is the image of the Church as the Bride of Christ. This metaphor not only encapsulates the intimate and sacrificial nature of the bond between Christ and the Church but also underscores the pivotal role of the Incarnation in shaping the Church's identity and mission.

The concept of the Church as the Bride of Christ is deeply embedded within the fabric of the New Testament. Ephesians 5:25-27 offers a seminal articulation of this metaphor, as Paul draws a parallel between the love of Christ for the Church and the love of a husband for his wife: "*Husbands, love your wives, as Christ loved the church and gave Himself up for her, to sanctify and cleanse her with the washing of water by the word, that He might present her to Himself a glorious church, not having spot or wrinkle or any such thing, but that she should be holy and without blemish*" (ESV). This passage underscores the sacrificial love of Christ, who gave Himself up for the Church, purifying and sanctifying her. The analogy emphasizes the depth of Christ's commitment and the transformative effect of His love on the Church.

Revelation 19:7-9 further develops this imagery, presenting the Church as the "*bride of the Lamb*": "*Let us rejoice and be glad and give Him glory! For the marriage of the Lamb has come, and His wife has made herself ready. And it was granted to her to be arrayed in fine linen, bright and pure—for the fine linen is the righteous acts of the saints.*" This eschatological vision symbolizes the ultimate consummation of the divine union, a moment of unparalleled joy and fulfillment for the Church. It encapsulates the Church's hope and longing for its final union with Christ.

To fully comprehend the depth and significance of the Church as the Bride of Christ, one must delve into the heart of Christian theology: the Incarnation. This pivotal doctrine asserts that Jesus Christ, the eternal Son of God, assumed human nature, becoming fully human while remaining fully divine.

As John proclaims, "*And the Word became flesh and dwelt among us, and we have seen His glory, glory as of the only begotten from the Father, full of grace and truth*" (John.1:14). This transformative event marked the beginning of a new era and laid the foundation for the Church. The Incarnation is not merely a historical event but an on-going reality that continues to shape the Church's identity and mission.

The Incarnation establishes a profound connection between the divine and the human, with Christ as the head of the Church. As Paul emphasizes in Colossians 1:18, Christ is the "*head of the body, the church.*" This relationship underscores the Church's dependence on Christ and its role as an extension of His redemptive work. Through this divine-human union, the Church is intricately connected to Christ, receiving nourishment, guidance, and purpose from Him.

Furthermore, the Church is often depicted as the Body of Christ, a metaphor that highlights the organic unity of believers. Just as the human body functions as a harmonious whole, so too does the Church. The Incarnation provides the foundational blueprint for this unity, as Christ, through His death and resurrection, reconciled humanity to God. This concept is beautifully expressed by Paul in 1 Corinthians 12:27, "*Now you are the body of Christ, and each one of you is a part of it.*" The Body of Christ metaphor underscores the interconnectedness and mutual support among believers, reflecting the unity established through Christ's Incarnation.

The Incarnation also paved the way for the Church to become the dwelling place of the Holy Spirit. As Paul declares in 1 Corinthians 3:16, believers are "*God's temple.*" The indwelling of the Holy Spirit transforms the Church into a living sanctuary, empowered to carry out its mission. This transformation is a direct result of the Incarnation, as the Holy Spirit's work builds upon the foundation laid by Christ's incarnation. The presence of the Holy Spirit within the Church empowers believers for service, fostering spiritual growth and deepening their relationship with God.

Moreover, the Incarnation ushered in a new creation, a world transformed by the grace of God. The Church embodies this new reality, a community of believers who have been renewed in Christ. As Paul states in 2 Corinthians 5:17, *"Therefore, if anyone is in Christ, he is a new creation. The old has gone, behold, the new has come."* This new creation is characterized by a restored relationship with God and a renewed sense of purpose and mission.

The early Church Fathers offered profound insights into the Church's identity and its connection to the Incarnation. St. Augustine, for instance, in his monumental work *On the Trinity* 7, 5, provides a rich theological reflection on the Church as the Body of Christ. Augustine emphasizes the unity and nourishment provided by Christ's Incarnation, underscoring the Church's dependence on Christ as its life-giving source. He writes, *"The Church is the Body of Christ, and in that Body, the Incarnation is the source of its unity and life."*

St. John Chrysostom, in his *Homilies on Ephesians*, Hom.21, eloquently describes the intimate union between Christ and the Church, comparing it to the bond between a husband and wife. He highlights Christ's role in sanctifying the Church, emphasizing His transformative love. Chrysostom states, *"Christ loves the Church with a love that surpasses all understanding, a love that sanctifies and transforms her into a glorious bride."*

St. Cyril of Alexandria, in his Commentary on the Gospel of John 11,3, underscores the role of the Holy Spirit in sanctifying the Church members and uniting them with Christ, the Head of the Body. His reflections on the Incarnation and its implications for the Church offer invaluable insights into the early Church's understanding of the relationship between Christ and His Body. Cyril notes, "*The Holy Spirit works through the Church to sanctify its members and to unite them with Christ, who is the Head of the Body.*"

Therefore, The imagery of the Church, when viewed through the lens of the Incarnation, reveals a rich and multifaceted tapestry. The Incarnation, as the foundational event, gave birth to the Church and continues to shape its identity, mission, and destiny. It is through the Incarnation that the Church finds its purpose, its unity, and its hope. This profound relationship between Christ and the Church, marked by sacrificial love and divine grace, underscores the transformative power of the Incarnation and its ongoing impact on the life of the Church.

Part Three
Understanding the Christian Doctrine of Incarnation:
Distinctions, Development, and Context

This part, titled "*Understanding the Christian Doctrine of Incarnation: Distinctions, Development, and Context*," seeks to elucidate the complex and multifaceted nature of this doctrine, examining its unique characteristics, historical evolution, and its place within the broader religious and philosophical landscape.

We begin by exploring "*The Distinct Nature of the Christian Doctrine of the Incarnation*," where we will identify what sets Christian teachings apart from other religious traditions regarding divine embodiment. This discussion will highlight the foundational principles that define the Incarnation and its significance within Christianity.

In "*The Insufficiency of Linguistic Similarities*," we will address the limitations of drawing parallels between Christian concepts and those found in other religious systems. While linguistic similarities may suggest connections, they often fail to capture the depth and specificity of Christian theological claims.

The part then turns to "*Theological Distinctions in the Doctrine of the Incarnation*," providing an in-depth analysis of how Christian understandings of Incarnation diverge from those of other traditions. This section will explore key theological arguments that underscore the uniqueness of the Christian doctrine.

Next, "*Theological Continuity and Development*" will trace the historical and theological evolution of the Incarnation doctrine within Christianity. This examination will illustrate how Christian thought on Incarnation has developed over time, reflecting changes in doctrinal understanding and context.

We will also consider "*Judaism and Paganism*," investigating how the Christian doctrine of the Incarnation interacts with and diverges from the religious beliefs of ancient Judaism and pagan traditions. This comparison will shed light on the historical and cultural influences that have shaped Christian theology.

The discussion will then move to "*Rationality and Faith*," where we will explore the relationship between reason and belief in the context of the Incarnation. This section will delve into how faith in the Incarnation intersects with rational thought and philosophical inquiry.

Finally, "*Prayer and Incarnation*" will examine the impact of the doctrine of the Incarnation on Christian practices of prayer. We will explore how the belief in God's embodiment influences and transforms the way Christians engage in prayer and worship.

Through this comprehensive exploration, we aim to provide a nuanced understanding of the Christian doctrine of the Incarnation, highlighting its distinctiveness, historical development, and its broader implications for faith and practice.

The Distinct Nature of the Christian Doctrine of the Incarnation

Recent readings have suggested that the doctrine of the Incarnation is borrowed from pagan religions. Such claims require thorough examination to determine their validity. Several key points must be considered. Firstly, these criticisms often lack substantive evidence and fail to provide concrete comparisons between pagan texts and biblical scriptures to substantiate claims of borrowing or imitation. For instance, the New Testament extensively references Old Testament prophecies, which Christians believe foretell the coming of Jesus Christ.

A notable example is Isaiah 7:14, which states, *"Therefore the Lord himself will give you a sign: The virgin will conceive and give birth to a son, and will call him Immanuel."* This prophecy is central to the Christian doctrine of the Incarnation, and its fulfilment is explicitly connected in the New Testament. In Matthew 1:22-23, it is written, *"All this took place to fulfill what the Lord had said through the prophet: 'The virgin will conceive and give birth to a son, and they will call him Immanuel' (which means 'God with us')."* This linkage highlights that the doctrine of the Incarnation is firmly rooted in Jewish scriptural traditions rather than in pagan beliefs.

Another significant prophecy is found in Micah 5:2, which states, *"But you, Bethlehem Ephrathah, though you are small among the clans of Judah, out of you will come for me one who will be ruler over Israel, whose origins are from of old, from ancient times."* This prophecy is cited in Matthew 2:5-6 when the chief priests and scribes inform King Herod of the Messiah's birthplace, reinforcing that the Incarnation doctrine is tied to Jewish prophetic traditions. In addition, the Old Testament includes prophecies that Christians believe are fulfilled in the life of Jesus, such as those found in Isaiah 53, which describes the suffering servant who bears the sins of many. Isaiah 53:5 reads, *"But he was pierced for our transgressions, he was crushed for our iniquities; the punishment that brought us peace was on him, and by his wounds we are healed."* This chapter is frequently cited in the New Testament to explain the purpose of Jesus' suffering and death, indicating a deep connection between Old Testament prophecy and New Testament teachings.

Secondly, it is crucial to remember that Christianity emerged in Palestine within a Jewish context. If Christianity had originated in Babylon, Egypt, or Persia, it might be reasonable to question its origins. However, Christianity's emergence in a Jewish setting provides a different context. The New Testament reflects this Jewish background consistently. The Apostle Paul, in his Epistle to the Romans 1:2, asserts, *"The gospel he promised beforehand through his prophets in the Holy Scriptures."*

This reference underscores that the Christian gospel, including the doctrine of the Incarnation, is based on Jewish scriptural foundations. Paul's epistles frequently refer to the Jewish scriptures to explain Christian teachings, demonstrating that early Christianity was deeply rooted in Jewish tradition.

Furthermore, both the Old and New Testaments actively oppose paganism. The First Commandment in Exodus 20:3 states, *"You shall have no other gods before me,"* which firmly opposes the worship of other deities. This command is reinforced throughout the Old Testament, including in Deuteronomy 6:14: *"Do not follow other gods, the gods of the peoples around you."* The New Testament continues this opposition, as seen in 1 John 5:21: *"Dear children, keep yourselves from idols."* The clear stance against idolatry and pagan worship in these scriptures highlights the inconsistency of claims that Christian doctrines like the Incarnation are borrowed from paganism. Additionally, claims that ancient Egyptians were aware of concepts such as the Trinity, the Incarnation, or the cross lack substantial evidence. Such claims often reflect more about the agendas of those making the claims rather than about historical facts.

Addressing the comparison with the Christian Trinity, equating it with Egyptian deities like Osiris, Horus, and Isis is unfounded. The Egyptian mythological triad, often including Set, does not align with the Christian concept of the Trinity. For example, Osiris, Horus, and Isis, as depicted in the *"Pyramid Texts"* and the *"Book of the Dead,"* are part of a pantheon that includes Set, a deity associated with chaos and disorder. The distinctiveness of the Christian Trinity is emphasized by early Church Fathers highlighting the unique nature of the Christian understanding of God's relationship with humanity.

Moreover, the term *"hell"* in ancient religions, found in texts like the *"Book of the Dead,"* refers to the underworld and the realm of the dead but differs significantly from the Christian concept of hell as a place of eternal punishment.

For instance, Matthew 25:46 states, *"Then they will go away to eternal punishment, but the righteous to eternal life,"* describing hell in terms of eternal consequences for the wicked. This difference in connotation underscores that similar terms do not necessarily indicate a direct adoption of religious concepts.

Addressing claims that Pharaohs were considered incarnations of deities, there is a significant difference between this and the Christian doctrine of the Incarnation. Christianity asserts that God Himself became incarnate in Jesus Christ once and for all, a unique event central to Christian theology. Early Church Father Irenaeus of Lyons emphasizes this distinction in his work *Against Heresies* 3. 16, stating, *"The Word became flesh to offer humanity a complete and perfect salvation."* This statement underscores the unique nature of the Incarnation, which involves the full revelation of God through Jesus Christ, contrasting with the Egyptian belief where Pharaohs were seen as divine rulers rather than direct incarnations of the divine essence. Historical texts such as "*The Royal Canon of Turin*" depict Pharaohs as divinely favored rulers but not as embodiments of divine nature.

Further elaboration from early Church Fathers supports the distinctive nature of the Incarnation. Tertullian, in *Against Praxeas* 27, argues that the Incarnation is a unique doctrine of Christianity, emphasizing the Christian belief in a personal and direct revelation of God. He writes, *"The Christian belief that God became man is not to be confused with the mythological gods of paganism, who were mere manifestations of the divine in different forms."* Similarly, in *On the Unity of the Church.* 1, Cyprian of Carthage asserts the uniqueness of the Incarnation, saying, *"Christ, the Son of God, became incarnate to reconcile humanity with God, a mystery distinct from any pagan ritual or myth."*

The Christian understanding of the Incarnation is also affirmed by Athanasius in his *Letters to Serapion Letter 1. 8*, where he explains that the doctrine of the Incarnation is not borrowed from pagan sources but is a fundamental truth of Christian faith, stating, *"The mystery of the Incarnation is a divine act that surpasses all human understanding and is rooted in the revelation given by Christ."* This assertion reinforces the view that the Incarnation is a unique Christian doctrine, not derived from pagan traditions.

Christianity's doctrine of the Incarnation is distinctive in emphasizing God's full revelation through Jesus Christ. This doctrine reflects a unique and profound theological understanding, different from the more superficial divine associations found in ancient beliefs. The Incarnation in Christianity is not merely about divine endorsement of earthly rulers but about God revealing His very nature and love for humanity through Jesus.

While historical and linguistic parallels between pagan and Christian beliefs can be intriguing, they should not overshadow the profound theological differences that distinguish Christian doctrine from pagan religions. The Incarnation remains a unique and central doctrine of Christianity, firmly rooted in Jewish prophecy and Christian theology, rather than in pagan traditions.

The Insufficiency of Linguistic Similarities

When examining textual similarities between different works, it is crucial to understand that mere linguistic resemblance does not necessarily imply direct borrowing or influence. For instance, texts written in different places and by different authors, separated by time, may exhibit similar expressions or ideas, which does not inherently mean that one work is influenced by another. An illustrative example of this can be found in the proverbial wisdom shared across various cultures.

The adage that "*lying is short-lived*" appears in different cultures, suggesting that such similarities may arise from a common human understanding of moral truths rather than direct imitation. This notion is evident in the Proverbs of Solomon, which stress the consequences of dishonesty. Proverbs 12:19 states, *"Truthful lips endure forever, but a lying tongue lasts only a moment,"* which reflects a universal acknowledgment of the ephemeral nature of deceit.

Human wisdom often transcends specific cultures or historical contexts. Common proverbs or sayings may emerge independently in various cultures because they encapsulate universal human experiences and observations.

The ancient Greek philosopher Socrates, for instance, is famously quoted as saying, *"An unexamined life is not worth living"* (Plato's "Apology," 36c). This reflects a fundamental human insight into the value of self-awareness and integrity, which resonates with similar sentiments in ancient Near Eastern texts. For example, the Sumerian proverb *"He who tells the truth is always wise"* echoes the same value of honesty found in Proverbs.

The crucial aspect is not merely the presence of similar phrases but the theological context in which they are used. Descriptions of divine attributes in various religions might use similar language, but the underlying theological implications can differ significantly. For instance, the sun is often deified in ancient Egyptian religion, as seen in the worship of Ra, the sun god, who is depicted as the supreme deity with immense power. In the *"Book of the Dead,"* Chapter 17, Ra is described as having a crucial role in the afterlife, *"Ra, the great god, who lives upon truth, who is mighty, who is in the boat of the sun."* This deification contrasts sharply with the Christian understanding of divine omnipotence. In Christianity, the sun is considered a creation of God rather than a deity itself. The New Testament reinforces this view, as illustrated in John 1:3, which states, *"Through him all things were made; without him nothing was made that has been made."* This passage underscores that while the sun and other elements are part of God's creation, they are not objects of worship.

Early Church Fathers emphasized the unique nature of Christian doctrine compared to pagan beliefs. Irenaeus of Lyons, in *Against Heresies* 1. 22, writes, *"The Scriptures have clearly shown that the creation is distinct from the Creator, and we must not confuse the created order with the divine essence."* This assertion emphasizes the clear separation between the Creator and creation, countering any potential conflation with pagan deities.

This reflects a unique aspect of Christian theology where the Incarnation represents God's direct intervention in human history for the purpose of salvation, rather than borrowing from or resembling pagan myths.

Similarly, Augustine of Hippo in *Confessions* 12. 10 addresses the nature of divine creation and its distinction from pagan worship practices. Augustine states, *"The creation is a testimony to the Creator's majesty, not an object of worship in itself."* This distinction reinforces the Christian view that while natural elements like the sun are part of God's creation, they are not divine in themselves and are not to be worshipped.

The use of similar language or symbols in various religious contexts does not necessarily indicate a direct influence or borrowing but rather reflects a shared human effort to articulate complex ideas about the divine and moral order. The Christian doctrine, as articulated by early Church Fathers and supported by biblical texts, maintains a clear distinction between the Creator and creation, emphasizing a unique understanding of divine attributes and salvation that is not derived from pagan traditions. This perspective is essential for understanding the distinctive nature of Christian theology and its separation from other religious or cultural practices.

Theological Distinctions in the Doctrine of the Incarnation

Turning back to the doctrine of the Incarnation, it is essential to address concerns about its perceived similarity to pagan concepts. The Incarnation in Christianity involves God becoming human to reveal Himself, an event unique in its nature and purpose. This is markedly different from pagan beliefs, which often involve deities endowing human rulers with divine power. For example, in the ancient Roman world, emperors such as Augustus were deified posthumously to legitimize their successors and consolidate political power. This practice is documented by Suetonius in *"The Twelve Caesars,"* where he writes about Augustus's deification, noting that the Senate officially deified him after his death to secure his political legacy (*Suetonius, "The Twelve Caesars," Augustus* 98).

In contrast, the Christian doctrine of the Incarnation is described as God taking on human form not to grant divine status to a human being, but to elevate humanity itself. This act of divine condescension is meant to offer salvation and transformation to believers, rather than merely reinforcing the authority of a ruler. The Gospel of John encapsulates this unique aspect of the Incarnation, stating in John 1:14, *"The Word became flesh and made his dwelling among us. We have seen his glory, the glory of the one and only Son, who came from the Father, full of grace and truth."* This passage highlights the distinctiveness of the Incarnation as a divine act of self-revelation, contrasting sharply with the nature of pagan divine manifestations, which were often intended to support political power rather than effectuate spiritual transformation.

The theological implications of the Incarnation are further clarified in the Epistle to the Hebrews. Hebrews 2:14-17 explains, *"Since the children have flesh and blood, he too shared in their humanity so that by his death he might break the power of him who holds the power of death — that is, the devil — and free those who all their lives were held in slavery by their fear of death."*

This passage reflects the Christian belief that the Incarnation was a means to address the human condition directly, offering a path to spiritual renewal and freedom from the fear of death. This contrasts with pagan notions where divine status granted to rulers was typically limited to their earthly reign and did not entail a transformation of human nature itself.

The early Church Fathers emphasized this distinction between the Incarnation and pagan deification. Irenaeus of Lyons, in *Against Heresies* 3. 16, also clarifies the purpose of the Incarnation. He writes, *"The Word of God, through whom all things were made, became incarnate for the purpose of restoring what had been corrupted by sin."* This emphasizes that the Incarnation was not about political power or divine endorsement of earthly rulers but about restoring humanity to its original state of grace.

Augustine of Hippo, in *City of God* 11.10, further distinguishes the Christian doctrine from pagan practices. He writes, *"The Incarnation of Christ was not for the purpose of deifying mankind as pagan gods were deified, but to redeem and transform humanity."* Augustine's work underscores the distinctiveness of Christian theology, focusing on salvation and the elevation of human nature through divine grace rather than the symbolic or political divine status found in paganism.

The Christian understanding of the Incarnation also contrasts sharply with the deification of rulers in pagan traditions, which often served to reinforce political authority rather than to transform the human condition. For instance, in Egyptian religion, pharaohs were seen as divine beings or manifestations of gods like Horus or Ra.

This divine status was intended to support their political authority and maintain cosmic order, as described in the "*Pyramid Texts*" (*Utterance* 273), which proclaims, *"The king is Horus, the great falcon, the lord of the two lands."* This divine kingship was a political tool rather than a transformative spiritual act.

In summary, while superficial similarities between Christian and pagan concepts might exist, the doctrine of the Incarnation is fundamentally distinct. Pagan deification often reinforced political authority, whereas the Christian Incarnation represents a profound act of divine self-revelation and salvation, intended to elevate humanity and offer eternal life. The teachings of early Church Fathers and biblical texts collectively highlight the unique nature of the Incarnation as a transformative event with a purpose far beyond the political or symbolic deification seen in pagan traditions.

Theological Continuity and Development

The concept of human deification in Christianity is distinct from the deification of individual rulers in pagan contexts, reflecting a unique theological development with profound implications for understanding divine-human interaction. Christianity emphasizes the transformation of human nature through divine grace rather than merely elevating an individual to a divine status. This transformation is rooted in the doctrine of the Incarnation, which signifies a radical and unprecedented event in religious history.

In Christian doctrine, the Incarnation is described as God becoming human to effectuate salvation and elevate humanity. This is fundamentally different from the deification of rulers in pagan traditions, where such deification often served to legitimize political authority rather than to transform human nature. For example, the Roman practice of deifying emperors like Augustus was largely a political manoeuvre.

Augustus was deified posthumously, and Suetonius in *"The Twelve Caesars"* details how the Senate officially deified Augustus to support the political stability of his successors: *"Augustus was declared a god by the Senate"* (*Suetonius, "The Twelve Caesars," Augustus* 98). This practice was intended to reinforce the political legitimacy of the emperor's rule rather than to affect a spiritual transformation.

In contrast, Christian deification involves a profound theological shift. The New Testament teaches that through the Incarnation, God did not merely confer divine status upon Jesus but engaged in a transformative act that elevates human nature. This concept is reflected in 2 Peter 1:4, which states, *"Through these he has given us his very great and precious promises, so that through them you may participate in the divine nature, having escaped the corruption in the world caused by evil desires."* This passage highlights that the purpose of the Incarnation is not to elevate an individual for political reasons but to enable all believers to partake in the divine nature. The distinction between Christian and pagan deification becomes even clearer when considering the practices of ancient Egyptian religion.

Pharaohs were often seen as divine or semi-divine beings, which was intended to reinforce their political authority and maintain cosmic order. For example, the *"Pyramid Texts"* (*Utterance* 273) state, *"The king is Horus, the great falcon, the lord of the two lands."* This description serves to consolidate the ruler's authority and legitimize their reign, rather than to transform human nature.

The pagan practice of deifying rulers was also evident in ancient Greece, where figures like Alexander the Great were deified to legitimize their rule. Diodorus Siculus, in *"Library of History"* (*Book XVII*), notes that after Alexander's death, he was worshiped as a god: *"The Greeks, following the custom of their ancestors, honoured Alexander as a deity."* This practice, similar to that in Rome, was intended to reinforce political power and legacy rather than to effect a spiritual transformation.

In contrast, the Christian doctrine of the Incarnation focuses on spiritual renewal and transformation .Augustine's assertion emphasizes that the goal of the Incarnation is the redemption and elevation of humanity to a new state of grace, contrasting with the political or symbolic deification seen in paganism.

Additionally, the New Testament's integration of Jewish prophecy and teachings further distinguishes Christian deification from pagan practices. For example, Jesus' reference to fulfilling the Law and the Prophets in Matthew 5:17 indicates a continuation and expansion of earlier religious concepts: *"Do not think that I have come to abolish the Law or the Prophets; I have not come to abolish them but to fulfil them."* This fulfilment of Jewish prophecy demonstrates how Christianity builds upon its roots while presenting a new understanding of divine-human interaction.

In summary, while there may be superficial similarities between Christian and pagan concepts of deification, the fundamental nature and purpose of Christian doctrine are distinct. The Incarnation represents a transformative act of divine grace intended to elevate humanity and offer spiritual renewal, rather than simply conferring divine status for political or symbolic reasons. The teachings of the New Testament, combined with the writings of early Church Fathers, underscore the unique and profound nature of Christian theology and its departure from earlier pagan practices.

Judaism and Paganism

Expanding on the relationship between Judaism and pagan religions, particularly ancient Egyptian paganism, involves a thorough exploration of the distinctions and similarities between these traditions. The argument that if Judaism were fundamentally pagan, it would be understandable for elements of paganism to persist in Christianity, necessitates a closer examination of the theological and historical contexts. This discussion must address the claims with a careful consideration of biblical texts and early Christian writings.

The Old Testament, the core of Jewish religious heritage, presents a theological framework markedly different from the polytheistic beliefs of ancient Egypt. For example, the central tenet of monotheism in Judaism is unequivocally stated in Deuteronomy 6:4: *"Hear, O Israel: The LORD our God, the LORD is one."* This declaration underscores the belief in a single, all-powerful God, contrasting sharply with the polytheistic Egyptian religion, where deities were often associated with natural phenomena and aspects of life.

Further illustrating the distinct nature of Jewish theology, the creation narrative in Genesis 1 describes a single, omnipotent God creating the universe: *"In the beginning God created the heavens and the earth"* (Gen.1:1).

This narrative emphasizes God's sovereignty and intentionality in creation, which stands in contrast to the Egyptian creation myths, where multiple gods were involved in the creation process, such as in the Heliopolitan creation myth where Atom is a key figure in creating other gods and the world.

The practice of prayer in Judaism, while also present in other ancient cultures, is deeply rooted in a monotheistic context. The Hebrew Bible describes various forms of prayer and supplication, such as in Psalm 51:17: *"The sacrifices of God are a broken spirit; a broken and contrite heart, O God, you will not despise."* This reflects the Jewish emphasis on sincere, personal communication with God rather than the ritualistic or political aspects of pagan practices.

Fasting is another practice mentioned in the Old Testament, specifically in Leviticus 16:29-30: *"This is to be a lasting ordinance for you: On the tenth day of the seventh month you must deny yourselves and not do any work...because on this day atonement will be made for you to cleanse you."* This practice of fasting as a means of atonement and purification is an integral part of Jewish worship, distinct from the ritual fasting seen in Egyptian religion, which was often linked to various gods and the pharaoh's divine status.

The early Christian writers and Church Fathers made significant efforts to differentiate Christian doctrines from pagan beliefs. For instance, Irenaeus of Lyons in his seminal work *Against Heresies* 1. 10

addresses the distinctiveness of Christian teaching: *"The tradition of the apostles, which is manifest in all the churches, is consistent with the teachings we follow. It does not align with the fables of pagan religions."* This quote highlights the claim that Christian doctrine, while recognizing certain universal elements, remains distinct due to its unique theological assertions.

Our belief is not about elevating an individual to divine status but about redeeming and transforming human nature. This differentiation underscores the transformative nature of Christian doctrine, which aims to elevate human nature through divine grace rather than through ritual or political means.

The role of specialized religious practitioners, such as priests, in both Judaism and pagan religions reflects a common aspect of human societies. However, the function and purpose of these roles vary significantly. In ancient Israel, priests were tasked with maintaining the covenant relationship between God and His people, performing sacrifices, and upholding religious laws as described in books like Leviticus. This role is distinct from the Egyptian priesthood, which was intertwined with the political and social structure of the state and often served to reinforce the divine authority of the pharaoh.

In conclusion, while there are similarities in religious practices across different cultures, such as prayer and fasting, these practices should be understood as universal expressions of human spirituality rather than indications of direct borrowing or imitation.

The theological foundations of Judaism and Christianity, as reflected in the Hebrew Bible and early Christian writings, highlight a unique and transformative understanding of divine-human relationships. The Christian doctrine, particularly the concept of the Incarnation, represents a distinctive development in religious thought that cannot be simply equated with the deification practices of ancient pagan religions.

Rationality and Faith

The observation that religious practices such as the roles of clergy, temples, prayer, fasting, and sacred texts are prevalent across ancient and contemporary religions raises an important question: if these practices reflect fundamental human needs for specialization, continuity, and responsibility, does this imply that they are purely human inventions and not divine in origin? This question delves into the relationship between human intellect and divine revelation, and whether these practices have a deeper, divinely inspired foundation or are merely human responses to existential needs.

Human reason is a gift from God, as the Bible states. When human intellect discovers something accurate or beneficial, it ultimately traces back to its divine source. Proverbs 2:6 notes, *"For the Lord gives wisdom; from his mouth come knowledge and understanding."* This indicates that human discoveries and insights are ultimately rooted in divine wisdom. This perspective is echoed in James 1:17, which says, *"Every good gift and every perfect gift is from above, coming down from the Father of lights."* Therefore, human achievements, including religious practices, are seen as part of God's overarching plan.

The notion that everything in human life must be directly ordained by God, including something as mundane as clothing, reflects a misunderstanding of the relationship between human invention and divine influence. The Bible does not assert that every human innovation is a direct command from God but rather that all good things are under His providence. For example, Acts 17:25 clarifies, *"Nor is he served by human hands, as if he needed anything. Rather, he himself gives everyone life and breath and everything else."* This suggests that while God provides for all things, human creativity and resourcefulness are also integral to His plan.

The dilemma arises when contemplating whether fundamental aspects of human relationship with God, such as prayer and fasting, are purely human inventions. This concern suggests that such practices might not be divinely revealed, potentially threatening faith and the integrity of religious doctrine. Early Christian writers addressed these concerns by affirming the role of human agency within divine revelation. For instance, Tertullian, in his *Apology* 9, argues that Christian practices, including prayer and fasting, are grounded in divine teaching but expressed through human traditions and adaptations. He states, *"We neither concede to you that our doctrine is derived from some origin in the books of the Chaldeans or Egyptians, nor from any ancient or new philosophies. Our doctrine is not of man's devising but of the Divine nature."*

The crux of this issue lies in a deeper skepticism toward human intellect, which can sometimes stem from a fear of freedom and a lack of trust in human capabilities as creations of God. It is essential to distinguish between human creations and divine acts. While human achievements, such as technological advancements, are celebrated for their utility and innovation, there is a tendency to view them separately from divine creations. Romans 12:6 supports this balance by stating, *"We have different gifts, according to the grace given to each of us."* This verse highlights that human gifts and achievements operate within the framework of divine grace.

Human intellect has been instrumental in discovering and utilizing various elements of the natural world, such as iron and its applications. Just as humans have used these discoveries to develop tools and technology, they also engage in practices like prayer, which can be seen as a means to connect with God.

The act of prayer, while universally practiced, may not necessarily be a divine prescription but rather a natural human response to a deeper existential need. Early Church Fathers like Origen in his *Commentary on Matthew* 10, 11 acknowledge that prayer is a response to divine invitation and necessity, rather than merely a human invention. Origen notes, *"Prayer is an expression of our need for God and is aligned with our nature to seek the divine."*

Prayer is a universal practice across cultures and religions. This widespread occurrence suggests that it is a general human experience rather than a specific divine command. Prayer, like other religious practices, serves as a form of communication and relationship between humans and the divine. The method of prayer and its frequency are left to human discretion, reflecting personal and cultural preferences rather than strict divine regulations. This adaptability is reflected in the New Testament. For instance, in Matthew 6:5-6, Jesus criticizes the practice of repetitive, mindless prayer typical of pagan religions: *"And when you pray, do not be like the hypocrites. For they love to pray standing in the synagogues and on the street corners to be seen by men. Assuredly, I say to you, they have their reward. But you, when you pray, go into your room, and when you have shut your door, pray to your Father who is in the secret place; and your Father who sees in secret will reward you openly."* Jesus emphasizes that genuine prayer should be sincere and personal, rather than ritualistic.

The Lord's Prayer, taught by Jesus, serves as a model rather than a rigid formula, allowing believers the freedom to express their spirituality within the framework of Christian teaching on incarnation. St. John Chrysostom, in his *Homilies on the Gospel of Matthew* 19, reflects on the Lord's Prayer as a guide for Christian conduct and communication with God. He writes, *"The Lord's Prayer is not a mere formula but a pattern that directs us to the depth of our relationship with God, showing us how to approach Him with sincerity and humility."*

Thus, while religious practices are shaped by human needs and cultural contexts, their spiritual significance remains deeply intertwined with the divine. They reflect an on-going dialogue between human experience and divine revelation, where both elements play a crucial role in the expression and understanding of faith. Early Church Fathers, such as Irenaeus in *Against Heresies* 4.5, affirmed that Christian practices, including prayer and fasting, are informed by divine revelation but adapted through human agency to express the relationship between humanity and God. Irenaeus states, *"The practices of the Church, including our prayers and fasts, are rooted in the divine teachings but are lived out through human experience, reflecting a harmony between God's will and our response."*

This perspective underscores the belief that while human practices may be influenced by cultural and historical factors, they are ultimately part of a divine plan that incorporates human creativity and experience.

Prayer and Incarnation

The relationship between prayer and the Incarnation is a profound aspect of Christian theology. The Incarnation represents a transformative event where God became human in the person of Jesus Christ, signifying a new approach to divine interaction and prayer. This pivotal doctrine suggests that prayer is no longer confined by ritualistic constraints but has become a continuous, intimate connection between humanity and the divine.

The New Testament highlights that prayer is to be a persistent and heartfelt communication with God. For instance, in 1 Thessalonians 5:17, Paul exhorts believers to *"pray without ceasing"* (1 Thess. 5:17, ESV), emphasizing that prayer should be an on-going part of life rather than limited to specific times or rituals. This notion contrasts sharply with the structured prayer times observed in many ancient pagan religions, where prayers were offered at designated hours, often bound by elaborate rituals.

The Incarnation, as described in the book of Hebrews, signifies a profound shift in how humanity approaches God. Hebrews 9:11-12 states: *"But when Christ appeared as a high priest of the good things that have come, then through the greater and more perfect tent (not made with hands, that is, not of this creation) he entered once for all into the holy places, not by means of the blood of goats and calves but by means of his own blood, thus securing an eternal redemption"* (Heb. 9:11-12, ESV). This passage illustrates that Christ's sacrifice has fulfilled and transcended previous ritualistic practices, including those related to prayer and purification.

Early Church Fathers such as St. Augustine reflect on the transformative nature of prayer in light of the Incarnation. In his *Confessions* 1.1, Augustine writes, "*You have made us for yourself, O Lord, and our hearts are restless until they rest in you*". This reflects the idea that prayer is an intrinsic part of the human condition, naturally oriented towards God.

The traditional practice of designated prayer times, such as the seven daily prayers, serves to guide spiritual growth rather than to impose rigid constraints. St. John Chrysostom, in his *Homily on Matthew* 7 acknowledges the flexibility in prayer practices: "*We are called to be constant in prayer, yet we should not be burdened by the strictness of a particular time or place*". This approach supports spiritual discipline while allowing for personal and cultural adaptation.

The question of whether paganism influenced Christianity is complex and requires careful historical and theological examination. Pagan religions, with their various rites and customs, existed long before Christianity. However, Christianity emerged within a Jewish context and drew upon Jewish traditions. Early Christian apologists such as Justin Martyr explicitly refuted the notion of pagan influence on Christian doctrine. In his *First Apology* 21 Justin Martyr states, "*For we have been taught that Christ is the firstborn of every creature, not like the gods of the pagans, who were born from their own kind*". This underscores the distinctiveness of Christian teachings.

The term "*Trinity*" in Christianity is another point of discussion. The doctrine of the Trinity should be understood within its own theological context rather than being compared superficially with pagan triads. Athanasius of Alexandria, in his *Four Orations Against the Arians* 3.3 emphasizes: "*The mystery of the Trinity is hidden from the understanding of the ungodly, but it is revealed through the Son*". This illustrates that Christian

Trinitarian theology is rooted in a unique revelation that differs from pagan conceptions.

In navigating religious studies and skepticism, it is essential to engage with both spiritual experience and rigorous scholarship. Personal spiritual experiences, such as the belief in Christ's sacrificial death for the redemption of sins, provide a foundation for faith that goes beyond theoretical analysis. Ignatius of Antioch, in his *Letter to the Smyrneans*, 8 highlights the importance of community: *"Where the bishop is present, there is the Church, just as where Christ is, there is the Catholic Church"*. This reflects the integral role of the Church in fostering and sustaining faith.

The idea that individuals are subject to fate, while the community operates according to established laws" emphasizes the stability of the Church compared to the fragility of individual lives. Cyprian of Carthage, in his *On the Unity of the Church* 6 reinforces this perspective: *"He cannot have God for his Father who does not have the Church for his mother"* .This statement underscores the importance of being part of a living, active faith community, where personal and communal aspects of faith are interwoven.

Navigating Faith and Community: Principles for a Transformative Christian Journey

In a world as complex and tangled as a dense forest, where numerous interpretations of Christian doctrine exist, finding a clear path can be challenging. To navigate this journey effectively, several foundational principles should guide our approach.

Firstly, diligent study is indispensable in the pursuit of faith and understanding. As the Apostle Paul instructed Timothy, *"Study to shew thyself approved unto God, a workman that needeth not to be ashamed, rightly dividing the word of truth"* (2 Tim 2:15, KJV). Engaging deeply with theological and philosophical texts allows believers to discern truth amidst diverse interpretations. Early Church Fathers like Augustine of Hippo and Origen of Alexandria emphasized the importance of rigorous study to uncover deeper spiritual meanings in Scripture.

Secondly, while knowledge is essential, spiritual experience plays a pivotal role in deepening faith. James exhorts believers not only to hear the word but to live it out: *"But be ye doers of the word, and not hearers only, deceiving your own selves"* (Jas 1:22, KJV). The Desert Fathers and Mothers of early monasticism exemplified this through their ascetic practices, demonstrating how personal encounter with God transforms theoretical knowledge into lived faith.

Thirdly, active participation in the church community is crucial for spiritual growth and mutual support.

The early Christians in Acts 2:42-47 devoted themselves to communal worship, fellowship, and prayer. Ignatius of Antioch, in his letters to various Christian communities, emphasized the importance of unity and obedience to the church leadership, highlighting how communal worship strengthens individual faith and guards against doctrinal deviations.

The tension between individual destiny and communal responsibility is a recurring theme in Christian thought. Individuals face vulnerabilities and uncertainties in life, whereas the church as a collective embodies endurance and resilience. Tertullian, a third-century theologian, addressed this dichotomy in his writings on the unity of the church, arguing that collective strength derives from shared faith despite individual weaknesses.

Moreover, the effectiveness of one's faith journey is not measured solely by personal achievements but by the transformative impact on society. Clement of Rome, in his First Epistle to the Corinthians, emphasized the virtue of humility and mutual respect within the church, advocating for a communal witness that influences societal ethics and values.

In conclusion, navigating the complexities of Christian faith and doctrine demands a balanced approach of rigorous study, spiritual experience, and active participation in the church community. This holistic journey not only deepens personal faith but also contributes to the collective witness of the church in society, reflecting the communal nature and mission of Christianity.

LOGOS ECHOES
WHEREVER LOGOS INSPIRE

Welcome To The Realm Of Logos

Where the profound realms of theology and spirituality intertwine, your journey of faith begins. Embark on a transformative quest for knowledge and spiritual growth as we offer a rich tapestry of E-books designed to nourish your soul and ignite your mind.

At the heart of Logos Echoes beats a passion for sharing the life-changing power of God's Word. We illuminate the timeless truths of Christianity with a fresh perspective, providing a captivating blend of deep theological insights and practical wisdom. By understanding the heart of God and the mind of Christ, we empower believers to live out their faith with confidence and purpose.

Our ministry is to ignite a flame within your heart, deepening your connection with Christ and equipping you to share His love with the world. Discover thought-provoking insights, practical guidance, and timeless truths that will transform your life, Through the life-changing message of Jesus Christ.

Together, we will unlock the boundless potential of your faith and experience the profound peace and fulfilment found in a deep relationship with Christ.

Waiting To Hear From You

If you find it worth it, please don't hesitate to contact us. Your feedback is like gold to us! These insights help us improve, grow, and create better Christian content for everyone. Share your thoughts and ideas with us. You are always welcome. And remember, our goal is:

**TOGETHER WITH LOGOS,
WE MAKE THE WORLD BETTER**

Email us: logosechoes@gmail.com

About the Author

Sameh Saied is A Researcher and Self-Published Author in the Field of Christian Studies, Particularly Focusing on the History of Early Christianity ,also the Founder of Logos Echoes Publications. His Aim is to Publish Works that address Theological, Biblical, and Spiritual Topics of interest to readers, to foster a deeper understanding of the Christian Faith, which is reflected in individual lives and society as a whole, by presenting diverse perspectives on the Bible and Christian Doctrines. Until now published four books:

- God Among Us: The Rational Case for the Incarnation.

- The Heart of Jesus: Unveiling His Eternal Love for Humanity.

- Restoring the Divine Participation: The Holy Spirit's Role and the Path to True Repentance.

- Recreating Humanity: Illuminating Our Divine Identity in Christ.

www.ingramcontent.com/pod-product-compliance
Lightning Source LLC
Chambersburg PA
CBHW071445130726
47997CB00006B/2238